THE INCREDIBLE
EDIBLE GIFTS
COOKBOOK

Revised Edition

Dona Z. Meilach

BRISTOL PUBLISHING ENTERPRISES
Hayward, California

A **nitty gritty**® cookbook

Printed in the United States of America.

ISBN 1-55867-300-8

Includes material previously published as *Gourmet Gifts,* ©1997, ISBN 1-55867-176-5

Cover design: Frank J. Paredes
Cover photography: ©Foodpix/Hagiwara
Food styling: Randy Mon
Illustrations: James Balkovek

CONTENTS

A book such as this, with its varied recipes and wide scope, requires myriad resources and friends who love to cook. I'm indebted to all who shared their favorite recipes with me. I especially want to thank Anne Machen and Barbara Morgenroth for their input and suggestions. But I believe my friends who willingly became testers should thank me for the boxes of goodies I supplied wherever and whenever we got together. I even brought cookies, candies, breads, honeys, curds and vinegars to the directors at the fitness club—going there was a necessary by-product of writing this book.

My thanks to my daughter, Susan Seligman, of Albuquerque, NM, whose comments are filled with wit, insight and humor. And thanks to my husband, Mel, who always appreciates the results of recipe testing.

Dona Meilach
Carlsbad, California

SAVE MONEY WITH INCREDIBLE EDIBLE GIFTS

This book is a compilation of recipes and fresh ideas for gifts that originate in the kitchen. The recipes are easy to whip up, whether you're a novice or an experienced cook. Countless items from specialty food stores and catalogs can be replicated in your own home at a fraction of the price. You will also find creative and money-saving ideas for packaging gifts in this book.

Give gourmet edible gifts to a host or hostess, a new neighbor, a sick friend or family member, a friend who just landed a new job, or a recent graduate. Or, offer homemade gifts to celebrate an anniversary, a new baby, a retirement, or any number of special occasions. Why not give an edible gift to a favorite friend, with a gift card that simply says, "Thinking of You" ?

Included in these pages are scores of ideas for both sweet and savory gourmet gifts. Cookies and candies, quick breads and yeast breads, jams and spreads come in a variety of guises. There are also unconventional gifts, such as dry spice blends and drink mixes, infused vinegars, flavored liqueurs and syrups and many more. When time is tight and you need a yummy gift in a hurry, become a "kitchen magician." Begin with ready-made foods, embellish them creatively and — presto! The result will wow your audience.

For extra appeal, package your edible gifts in attractive containers, festooned with ribbons and colorful tags. There are innovative wrapping ideas in this book, too, so that every present you give will be a pleasure to open.

Be careful to properly sterilize jars and bottles that will hold an edible gift. You'll find instructions in this book. Also, take care to state the storage information and shelf life of the item on the gift tag to ensure safety and quality. Mustards, syrups and dairy butters, especially, are highly perishable.

You'll love preparing and presenting gourmet edible gifts as much as your friends and family members will love receiving them. Even more, you'll adore all of the compliments. Soon you'll know that you can, indeed, make incredible edible gifts in your kitchen year-round.

BASICS

ABOUT FLOUR

All-purpose flour, bread flour and cake flour differ greatly, so make sure you are using the correct type for the recipe. Bread flour has a high gluten content and is important for achieving the right texture in yeast breads. All-purpose flour is used in quick bread and cookie recipes. Cake flour is made from very soft wheat and is used to make delicate items, such as cakes.

Avoid scooping flour directly from the bag with your measuring cup. To measure correctly, fluff up the flour in the bag or canister with a spoon before you spoon the flour lightly into a measuring cup. Don't tap or shake the cup to settle the flour. Instead, scrape excess flour from the top of the cup with a knife.

ABOUT YEAST

If you buy yeast in bulk, or don't use jars of it before the expiration date, store it in your freezer. Take out small amounts to thaw or keep in a small jar in the refrigerator until needed. Always let the measured amount of yeast warm to room temperature before using. For best results, use fast-acting (quick or bread machine) yeast. Fast-acting yeast doesn't call for proofing (dissolving in a warm liquid) before using; it can be mixed directly with the dry ingredients.

ABOUT COCOA POWDER

Look for "Dutch" or "Dutch process" cocoa powder, which is treated to neutralize cocoa's natural acidity. It will also impart a deep, rich chocolate flavor to your recipes.

ABOUT FREEZING

Freeze such items as cookies, bars and sliced breads between 2 layers of waxed paper in freezer containers. Or, separate items into individual portions and quick-freeze them on a baking sheet before packing in freezer containers.

HOW TO TOAST NUTS

Heat oven to 350°. Spread nuts evenly on an ungreased baking sheet and bake for 3 to 5 minutes, until nuts are slightly darkened and aromatic. Stir occasionally. Watch carefully so they don't burn.

HOW TO SOFTEN BUTTER

Let butter sit at room temperature until soft. Or, remove wrapper from butter, place on a plate and heat each stick in the microwave for up to 1 minute on LOW.

HOW TO MELT CHOCOLATE

Use packaged chocolate chips, baking chocolate or confectioners' chocolate for melting. Baking and confectioners' chocolate should be chopped into small pieces on a cutting board with a large serrated knife before melting.

On the stovetop, place chocolate chips or chopped chocolate in the top of a double boiler and melt over hot water, stirring frequently. If you don't have a double boiler, place chocolate in a heatproof glass or stainless steel bowl and place over a pot of hot water. Take care that the bottom of the bowl does not touch the water. Chocolate chips will take longer to melt than chopped chocolate.

In the microwave, heat chocolate chips or chopped chocolate on MEDIUM for about 1 minute. Stir to blend.

For drizzling, melt chocolate in a small plastic bag in the microwave. Snip off a corner of the bag and drizzle the chocolate onto cookies, candies or other items.

For dipping, melt chocolate chips or chopped chocolate in a double boiler or microwave for 1 to 2 minutes. Gradually add a small amount of vegetable oil until mixture reaches dipping consistency. Different brands of chocolate will require different amounts of oil.

After dipping items in chocolate, place them on waxed paper and let them set for about 30 minutes at room temperature before refrigerating. This will prevent cloudiness. If you use confectioners' chocolate, you can omit the setting time.

HOW TO SPLIT A VANILLA BEAN

Place vanilla bean on a cutting board. With a small sharp knife, cut vanilla bean from end to end through the center to expose the small black seeds inside, in which most of the flavor is concentrated. It is not necessary to cut all the way through the bean.

HOW TO MAKE CLEAN SHAPES WITH COOKIE CUTTERS

Plan your cuts with care to yield the maximum amount of cuts from the dough. Dip the cookie cutter in cold water to prevent the dough from sticking to it. Turn or rotate cutters often.

HOW TO CUT THE FAT WHEN BAKING

Bake cookies on a nonstick baking sheet or a baking sheet lined with parchment paper or a reusable nonstick pan liner, which can be cut to fit any pan. See page 8 for information. To cut back on saturated fats, it is usually fine to substitute margarine for butter; however, select a margarine that is suitable for baking. Use a baking fat substitute in place of butter, such as *Wonderslim, Lighter Bake* or applesauce. Baked goods will be softer than those made with butter.

HOW TO STERILIZE AND SEAL BOTTLES AND JARS

All containers holding gifts of food should be heat-sterilized before filling. Use canning jars for preserving jellies, sauces and other perishable foods destined for long storage. Canning jars come with "screwbands," which can be reused; however, never reuse the lids. Once canning lids have been used, they will not form another secure seal. Sterilize jars and lids by running them through the dishwasher. Or, boil them gently for 10 minutes in a large pot of boiling water. Be sure to use enough water to completely cover jars. Leave them in the sealed dishwasher or water until ready to use.

Bottles for foods that do not require canning procedures, such as flavored vinegars and liqueurs, can be closed with tight-fitting corks or screw-on caps.

Canning jars need a vacuum seal to ensure the safety of the food you are giving. Jars should be filled to within $1/2$ to 1 inch of the top of the jar. Remove air bubbles by running a butter knife around the inside of the jar. Place the lids on the jars and screw on metal bands securely. Submerge jars completely in a large pot of boiling-hot water and let sit for 10 minutes, taking care that jars do not touch. Remove jars from water with tongs and set on a rack to cool, allowing some space between jars. When the contents are at room temperature, check the seal. If necessary, repeat the sealing process with a new lid.

RESOURCES

NONSTICK PAN LINERS
Teflon Bakeware Liners
DuPont
(800) 986-2857

Von Snedaker
12021 Wilshire Blvd., Ste. 231
Los Angeles, CA 90025
(213) 395-6365

CANDY-MAKING SUPPLIES
The Candy Factory
2530 Riverside Drive
North Hollywood, CA 91607
(818) 766-8220

CANNING AND FOOD STORAGE
Kerr
(800) 344-5377
USDA Meat and Poultry Hotline
(800) 535-4555

BAKING EQUIPMENT
The Chef's Catalog
215 Commercial Ave.
Northbrook, IL 60052
(800) 338-3232

Many companies have Internet sites. Check your World Wide Web search engine for companies such as *Gold Medal Flour, Fleischmann's Yeast, Red Star Yeast* (Universal Foods Corporation), *Kellogg's Cereals, Reynolds Wrap Release® Nonstick Aluminum Foil,* United States Government Department of Food and Health and others for more information.

COOKIES

PRESENTING COOKIES

- Present cookies in a classic cookie jar or canister.
- Arrange cookies carefully on a bread board, baking sheet or tray. Wrap with clear plastic wrap and dress up with ribbons.
- Pack cookies in interesting, colorful tins, such as lunch boxes, candy containers, tea canisters and collectible boxes.
- Line a new flower pot with brightly colored tissue paper. Fill the lined pot with cookies and wrap the pot with clear plastic wrap. Gather excess wrap at the top and secure with a festive bow.
- Give a set of coffee mugs or pretty glasses stuffed with homemade cookies.
- Package individually wrapped cookies in a decorative basket. If desired, add packages of hot cocoa mix, spiced coffee or other gifts from your kitchen.
- Arrange cookies on colorful plastic plates lined with doilies. Wrap with colored plastic wrap or cellophane, gather excess wrap at the top and secure with a ribbon.
- For more ideas, see *Presenting Bars and Squares,* page 27.

BASIC BUTTER COOKIES

Makes 36 to 72 , depending on size

These easy cookies can be used as the basis for any variety of shapes and decorative toppings. Colored icings, candy sprinkles, cinnamon sugar or nuts work well — use your imagination. A few raisins or chocolate chips can become the eyes and nose of a teddy bear or clown. You can vary the flavor by substituting different flavors of extract for the vanilla.

1 cup unsalted butter, softened
1/2 cup sugar
1 egg
1 tsp. vanilla, lemon or other flavor extract

3 cups all-purpose flour
1 tsp. baking powder
1/2 tsp. salt

With a food processor or electric mixer, cream butter with sugar. Add egg and extract and mix until smooth. In a bowl, combine flour, baking powder and salt; add to butter mixture. Pulse or mix on low speed until well blended. Remove dough from bowl, wrap with plastic wrap and refrigerate for at least 1 hour or up to 2 days. Keep unused dough refrigerated until needed.

Heat oven to 375°. Using 1/4 of the dough at a time, roll dough on a lightly floured work surface until 1/4-inch thick. Cut into desired shapes with cookie cutters. Place cookies on lightly greased baking sheets about 1 inch apart and bake for 12 to 15 minutes, until golden brown. Cool on wire racks.

CHOCOLATE BUTTER COOKIES Makes 36 to 72, depending on size

This dough makes wonderful chocolate cookies on its own, or use it as the basis for a variety of different toppings.

1 pkg. (6 oz.) semisweet chocolate chips
1 cup unsalted butter, softened
3/4 cup dark brown sugar, packed
1 egg

1 tsp. vanilla extract
3 cups all-purpose flour
1/3 cup unsweetened cocoa powder
1/2 tsp. salt

Melt chocolate chips (see page 4) and cool; set aside. With a food processor or electric mixer, cream butter with sugar. Add egg and vanilla and mix until smooth. Add melted chocolate and mix until thoroughly blended. In a small bowl, mix flour with cocoa powder and salt. Gradually add cocoa mixture to butter mixture and pulse or mix at low speed until well blended. Remove dough from bowl, wrap with plastic wrap and refrigerate for at least 2 hours or up to 2 days. Keep unused dough refrigerated until needed.

Heat oven to 375°. Using 1/4 of the dough at a time, roll dough between 2 sheets of waxed paper until 1/8-inch thick. Cut into desired shapes with cookie cutters. Place on lightly greased baking sheets about 1 inch apart. Bake for 9 to 10 minutes, until dry to the touch. Cool on wire racks.

CHOCOLATE-DIPPED CRESCENT COOKIES

Makes about 60

Popular crescent cookies are traditionally made with chopped almonds, but almonds may be omitted or other chopped nuts may be used instead.

3½ cups flour
1 tsp. baking powder
1 cup butter, softened
8 oz. cream cheese, softened
2 cups sugar
1 egg

1 tsp. vanilla
¼ tsp. almond extract
¼ cup finely chopped almonds

ICING
1 pkg. (11½ oz.) white or chocolate chips
½ cup powdered sugar

Combine flour and baking powder in a bowl and set aside. In a large bowl, cream butter and cream cheese. Add sugar and beat until fluffy. Add egg, vanilla and almond extract. Beat well. Gradually add flour mixture, beating after each addition. Divide dough into three balls, wrap in waxed paper and refrigerate overnight or until well chilled. Work dough into long rolls about 2 inches in diameter. Cut and form crescents, or, make balls and flatten with a fork. Place on an ungreased cookie sheet. Bake for 10 minutes at 350º. Cool before icing.

For icing, melt chips. Dip one end of each cooled cookie in melted chocolate. Let set. Sprinkle remaining part of the cookie with powdered sugar.

CHEWY OATMEAL RAISIN COOKIES

Using applesauce or a baking fat substitute produces a soft, moist cookie without the saturated fat that comes from real butter. For more information, see How to Cut the Fat When Baking, *page 6.*

½ cup brown sugar, packed
¼ cup granulated sugar
⅓ cup applesauce or baking fat substitute
   (see page 6)
1 egg
1 tsp. vanilla extract
¾ cup all-purpose flour

½ tsp. baking soda
¼ tsp. baking powder
½ tsp. cinnamon
½ tsp. salt
1½ cups quick-cooking oats (do not use
   instant)
¾ cup raisins

Heat oven to 375°. In a large bowl, beat sugars, applesauce, egg and vanilla until well blended with a wooden spoon or whisk. In a small bowl, combine flour, baking soda, baking powder, cinnamon and salt. Stir flour mixture into applesauce mixture until blended. Stir in oats and raisins. Drop dough by rounded tablespoonfuls onto baking sheets sprayed with non-stick cooking spray. Bake for 8 to 10 minutes, until the edges begin to brown. Cool on wire racks.

CRANBERRY DELIGHT SUGAR COOKIES

Makes about 48

Dried or coarsely chopped fresh cranberries add a festive red color to these cookies.

1 cup dried or coarsely chopped fresh
   cranberries
2 tsp. grated orange peel (zest)
1 cup toasted walnut pieces (see page 4)
1 cup unsalted butter, softened

1 cup sugar
$\frac{1}{2}$ tsp. salt
$\frac{1}{2}$ tsp. cinnamon
1 egg yolk
2 cups all-purpose flour

With a food processor, chop cranberries with orange peel until finely minced; set aside. Place walnuts in workbowl and pulse until chopped into small pieces. With an electric mixer, cream butter and $\frac{3}{4}$ cup of the sugar. Add salt and cinnamon and mix well. Add egg yolk and mix until blended. Add cranberry mixture and walnuts and beat until mixed. Slowly add flour and blend until incorporated. Roll dough into 3 or 4 cylinders about 1-inch thick. Wrap cylinders with plastic wrap and refrigerate for at least 2 hours or up to 2 days.

Heat oven to 350°. Remove dough from refrigerator, remove plastic wrap and cut dough into $\frac{1}{4}$-inch rounds. Place rounds 1 inch apart on parchment-lined baking sheets and sprinkle with remaining $\frac{1}{4}$ cup sugar. Bake for 10 to 12 minutes, until edges begin to turn golden brown. Alternate the position of baking sheets halfway through baking time. Cool on wire racks.

ALMOND POPPY SEED BISCOTTI

Makes about 30

These Italian cookies are baked twice, which makes them very crisp and perfect for dipping. In Italy they are traditionally dipped into coffee or dessert wine. Biscotti taste best when made a few days before they are to be eaten. They make the ultimate gift cookie because they stay fresh for a long time. Package biscotti in large jars, as they do in gourmet coffee shops. Or, wrap several together with clear plastic and pack in a basket along with dipping items, such as flavored coffee, hot chocolate mix, spiced tea or dessert wine. Biscotti can be stored in a jar at room temperature for several weeks or wrapped and frozen for several months.

3 eggs or 4 egg whites
3/4 cup sugar
1 tsp. grated fresh orange peel (zest)
1/2 tsp. vanilla extract
2 1/2 cups all-purpose flour
1 tsp. baking powder
1/2 tsp. baking soda
1/4 tsp. salt
1 cup coarsely chopped toasted almonds (see page 4)
2 tbs. poppy seeds

Heat oven to 325°. With a food processor or electric mixer, beat eggs with sugar until light and foamy. Beat in orange peel and vanilla. Add flour, baking powder, baking soda and salt and beat until smooth. Stir in almonds and poppy seeds until well mixed.

Divide dough in half. Shape each half into a loaf, about 3½ inches wide and ¾-inch high. Place loaves at least 4 inches apart on a lightly greased baking sheet. Smooth tops and sides of loaves with a rubber spatula or lightly oiled fingers. Bake for 30 minutes, or until tops are golden brown. Cool for 10 minutes.

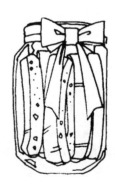

Reduce oven heat to 275°. Transfer loaves to a cutting board and cut each loaf diagonally into ½- to ¾-inch slices with a serrated knife. Place slices cut-side down on baking sheet and return to oven. Toast each side for about 10 minutes or until light golden brown. Cool completely before storing in airtight containers.

COCONUT WALNUT COOKIE BALLS

Makes about 36

These round cookies get extraordinary texture and flavor from coconut.

1 cup unsalted butter, softened
1/2 cup confectioners' sugar
2 tsp. coconut extract
2 cups all-purpose flour
2 cups finely chopped walnuts
1/2 cup flaked coconut
confectioners' sugar

Heat oven to 350°. In a large bowl, combine butter, 1/2 cup confectioners' sugar and coconut extract and mix with the back of a wooden spoon until blended. Gradually stir in flour, walnuts and flaked coconut until well mixed. Shape dough into 1-inch balls. Place balls on ungreased baking sheets and bake for 10 to 12 minutes, until firm, but not brown. Gently roll warm cookies in confectioners' sugar. Cool on wire racks.

MERINGUE "FORGOTTEN" COOKIES

Makes about 24

You can make these easy cookies and walk away from your oven for hours, or even overnight. The cookies bake after the oven is turned off and you've "forgotten" about them. Store in an airtight container at room temperature for up to 3 days or wrap and freeze for up to 2 months.

2 egg whites
$^2/_3$ cup sugar
1 tsp. vanilla extract
1 cup coarsely chopped pecans or walnuts
1 cup semisweet chocolate chips

Heat oven to 350°. In a medium bowl, beat egg whites until foamy. Gradually add sugar and vanilla and continue beating until stiff peaks form. Fold in nuts and chocolate chips. Drop teaspoonfuls of meringue mixture on a parchment-lined baking sheet. Place sheet in oven, turn off heat and leave in oven for at least 1 hour, or until cookies are completely cooled. Carefully remove cookies from parchment.

LIGHT CHOCOLATE COOKIES

Applesauce and egg whites work as fat replacements in these moist chocolate cookies. Decorate them with candy sprinkles for a festive look. Be sure the margarine you use is suitable for baking.

2¼ cups all-purpose flour
¼ cup unsweetened cocoa powder
1 tsp. cinnamon
½ tsp. ground cloves
1 tsp. baking soda
½ cup margarine

¾ cup sugar
2 egg whites
1½ cups applesauce or baking fat substitute (see page 6)
2 tbs. brewed coffee
1 cup plus 2 tbs. golden raisins

Heat oven to 350°. In a large bowl, stir together flour, cocoa, cinnamon, cloves and baking soda; set aside. In another large bowl, cream margarine and sugar with an electric mixer. Add egg whites and beat until well mixed. Beat in applesauce and coffee until well blended. Add flour mixture to applesauce mixture and stir until just mixed. Stir in raisins. Drop tablespoonfuls of dough about 2 inches apart on a nonstick baking sheet. Bake for about 10 to 15 minutes, or until tops are springy. Cool completely on a wire rack.

DOUBLE CHOCOLATE PISTACHIO COOKIE STICKS   Makes 60

These elegant, but easy, cookie sticks are covered with chocolate and dipped in finely chopped pistachio nuts.

2 tsp. grated lemon peel (zest)
2 cups finely chopped pistachio nuts
Chocolate Butter Cookie dough, page 12
8 oz. semisweet chocolate, chopped, melted (see page 4)

Stir grated lemon peel and 1 cup of the chopped pistachios into Chocolate Butter Cookie dough until thoroughly combined. Shape tablespoonfuls of dough into 2 x ½-inch sticks. Place on lightly greased baking sheets and bake for 9 to 10 minutes, until dry to the touch. Cool on wire racks.

While cookies are still slightly soft, dip ends of each cookie stick into melted semisweet chocolate; roll one end in remaining chopped pistachio nuts. Lay cookie sticks on waxed paper for about 30 minutes, until chocolate is set.

MAPLE OATMEAL COOKIES

This tasty, colorful variation on oatmeal cookies has a unique maple flavor.

2 cups all-purpose flour
1 cup sugar
1 tsp. salt
1 tsp. baking soda
2 tsp. pumpkin pie spice mix
2 cups quick-cooking oats

1 cup raisins
1 cup chopped pecans
2 eggs
3/4 cup melted butter
1/2 cup milk
2 tbs. maple flavoring

Heat oven to 350°. Prepare two baking sheets with nonstick spray coating or foil. In a large bowl, combine flour, sugar, salt, baking soda and pumpkin pie spice. Add oats, raisins and pecans; set aside.

In another large bowl, beat eggs. Add melted butter, milk and maple flavoring. Stir in flour mixture; mix well. Drop by teaspoonfuls onto greased cookie sheets. Bake for 15 minutes.

PUMPKIN-RAISIN DROPS

Makes about 24

Makes these for Thanksgiving and any time during the year. Pumpkin is so healthy that it is smart to learn to use it year round. Show your artistry when you decorate with ready-made icings. Customize your designs to the holiday or the person receiving the gift.

1 beaten egg	1 tsp. pumpkin pie spice
3/4 cup canned pumpkin	1/4 tsp. baking soda
1/3 cup brown sugar	1/4 tsp. salt
1 tbs. vegetable oil	1/4 cup raisins
1 tsp. vanilla	Prepared icings in different colors
3/4 cup all-purpose flour	

Prepare a baking sheet with nonstick spray or foil. In a medium mixing bowl, stir together egg, pumpkin, brown sugar, oil and vanilla. In a small mixing bowl, stir together flour, pumpkin pie spice, baking soda and salt. Add dry ingredients to pumpkin mixture. Stir in raisins. Drop the dough by rounded teaspoonfuls 1 inch apart onto cookie sheet. Bake in a 350° oven for 12 to 14 minutes, or until desired doneness. Cool on a wire rack. Ice.

ENGLISH TOFFEE COOKIES

Sunshiny yellow cookies with bits of toffee are a perfect accompaniment with a cup of tea or a glass of milk.

1 cup sugar
3/4 cup butter, softened
1 egg
1 tsp. vanilla
2 cups all-purpose flour

1 1/2 tsp. baking powder
1/4 tsp. baking soda
3/4 cup English toffee bits or chips
sugar

Heat oven to 350°. Combine sugar, butter, egg and vanilla in a large mixing bowl. Beat at medium speed until creamy (about 1 to 2 minutes), scraping bowl often. With mixer at low speed, add flour, baking powder and baking soda. Beat until well mixed, about 1 to 2 minutes. Stir in toffee bits by hand. Shape dough into 1 inch balls. Roll in sugar. Place balls 2 inches apart onto an ungreased cookie sheet. Flatten each ball with the bottom of a glass to a 1 1/2 inch circle. Dip glass bottom in sugar if it sticks to dough. Bake for 9 to 10 minutes. Remove from oven and let cool.

CHERRY CHOCOLATE CASHEW COOKIES   Makes about 50

The cherry color with white chocolate makes these perfect for holiday giving.

1 cup butter or margarine, softened
3/4 cup granulated sugar
3/4 cup firmly packed brown sugar
2 eggs
1 tsp. vanilla extract
2 1/4 cups all-purpose flour

1 tsp. baking soda
1 package (10 oz.) vanilla milk chips, or 1 2/3
  cups coarsely chopped white chocolate
1 1/2 cups dried tart cherries
1 cup lightly salted cashews

Heat oven to 375°. In a large mixing bowl, combine butter, sugar, brown sugar, eggs and vanilla. Mix with electric mixer on medium speed until thoroughly mixed. Combine flour and baking soda; gradually add flour mixture to butter mixture. Stir in vanilla chips or white chocolate; add dried cherries and cashew. Drop by rounded tablespoonfuls onto two ungreased baking sheets. Bake for 12 to 15 minutes, or until golden brown. Cool on a wire rack. Store in tightly covered containers.

BARS AND SQUARES

PRESENTING BARS AND SQUARES

- Present bars and squares in the pan in which they were baked. After bars have cooled, wrap the pan with clear or colored plastic wrap and decorate with brightly colored ribbons. For extra panache, include the recipe and a couple of cooking utensils, such as a spatula and an oven mitt, as part of the gift.

- For a dual-purpose gift, pack bars and squares into a reusable storage container with a tight-fitting lid. Gift recipients will remember your kindness every time they use the storage container.

- Place bars and squares in decorated brown paper bags (see page 145). Fold over tops, punch holes with a hole-punch and string colored yarn or ribbon through the holes.

- Pack bars or squares in a shiny gift bag lined with waxed paper.

- Cut bars and squares into small pieces and place each piece in a decorative paper candy cup. Pack in a decorative tin.

- Line the top and bottom of an empty candy box with wrapping paper, either purchased or homemade (see pages 147-149). Fill with individually wrapped bars or squares.

- For more ideas, see *Presenting Cookies,* page 10.

OATMEAL BARS WITH FRUITY FILLING

Use apricot, raspberry, strawberry or any other favorite jam for this recipe.

1 1/2 cups all-purpose flour
1 1/2 cups quick-cooking oats (do not use instant)
1 cup brown sugar, packed
1/2 tsp. baking soda
1/4 tsp. salt
5 tbs. applesauce
6 tbs. vegetable oil
1 cup jam

Heat oven to 350°. Spray a 9 x 13-inch pan with nonstick cooking spray. In a bowl, combine flour, oats, brown sugar, baking soda and salt. Add applesauce and oil and stir with a fork until mixture is evenly moist and crumbly.

Reserve 3/4 cup of the crumb mixture for topping. Press remaining crumb mixture evenly into prepared pan. Stir jam and spread thinly over crumb layer with a rubber spatula. Sprinkle reserved crumbs over jam and press gently. Bake for 25 to 30 minutes, until edges are golden. Cool and cut into bars.

LEAN AND LIGHT LEMON BARS

Makes 16

These have a delicious tang. Be sure to use a margarine that's suitable for baking.

3/4 cup all-purpose flour
1/4 cup margarine
2 tbs. reduced-fat sour cream
2 tbs. sugar
1 cup sugar
1 egg

2 egg whites
1 tbs. grated fresh lemon peel (zest)
3 tbs. fresh lemon juice
1/2 tsp. baking powder
1/4 tsp. salt
confectioners' sugar

Heat oven to 350°. Mix flour, margarine, sour cream and 2 tbs. sugar in a small bowl to form a dough. Pat dough in the bottom and 1/4 inch up the sides of an 8-inch square baking pan. Bake for about 20 minutes, until crust is lightly browned. Cool.

In a medium bowl, mix 1 cup sugar with egg, egg whites, lemon peel, lemon juice, baking powder and salt until well blended. Pour evenly over crust. Bake for about 20 to 25 minutes, until firm. Cool. Cut into bars and sprinkle lightly with confectioners' sugar.

PEAR-ORANGE BAR COOKIES

Fresh sliced pears in the middle layer of these easy-to-make bar cookies are a fruity surprise for the eye and the palate.

3 cups all-purpose flour
1 tsp. salt
1 cup vegetable shortening
1/2 cup milk
1/2 cup fine dry breadcrumbs
6 Bartlett pears, peeled, cored, sliced into 1/4-inch pieces
1/2 cup sugar
1 tsp. grated fresh orange peel (zest)
milk for brushing

GLAZE
1 cup confectioners' sugar, sifted
3/4 tsp. vanilla extract
2 tbs. orange juice or milk

Heat oven to 375°. In a large bowl, mix flour with salt. With a pastry blender or 2 knives, cut in shortening until mixture resembles coarse crumbs. Stir in milk, 1 tbs. at a time, until flour mixture is moistened.

On a lightly floured work surface, roll half of the dough into a 12 x 17-inch rectangle. Carefully place dough in a 10 x 15 x 1-inch baking pan, folding the dough edges up the sides of pan. Sprinkle dough with breadcrumbs. Arrange pear slices over crumbs. Combine sugar with orange peel and sprinkle over pear slices.

Roll remaining dough on a lightly floured work surface into a 10 x 15-inch rectangle; carefully place dough on top of pears. With the tines of a fork, press dough edges together to form a decorative seal. Cut several slits in top dough layer to allow steam to escape, and brush lightly with milk. Bake for 45 to 55 minutes, until top is golden brown.

Combine Glaze ingredients in a small bowl and stir until smooth. While still warm, brush glaze over top and carefully cut into bars.

FRUIT-NUT BARS

Make this delicious, fresh standby with raisins, blueberries, apricots, apples or cherries, too.

1¼ cups butter, softened
½ cup sugar
1 egg
½ cup molasses
½ cup milk
2 cups all-purpose flour
½ tsp. baking powder
½ tsp. baking soda

½ tsp. salt
1 cup nut pieces
1 cup chopped dried fruit

ICING
½ cup confectioners' sugar
1-2 tbs. milk
¼ tsp. lemon extract

Heat oven to 350°. In a bowl, beat butter, sugar, egg and molasses until well mixed. Stir in milk until blended. In another bowl, combine flour, baking powder, soda and salt; stir into butter mixture until well blended. Mix in nuts and dried fruit. Spread dough in a greased 9 x 13-inch pan. Bake for 20 to 25 minutes, until a slight imprint is left when top is touched lightly.

While bars are baking, combine icing ingredients in a small bowl and stir until smooth. Use only enough milk to achieve a drizzling consistency. With a spoon, drizzle icing over slightly cooled bars and cut into serving portions.

CHOCOLATE CHIP BARS

Makes 24 to 32

You can lighten this recipe a bit by using margarine instead of butter and egg whites instead of eggs. Be sure to use a margarine that's suitable for baking.

1/4 cup plus 2 tbs. butter or margarine, softened
1/3 cup granulated sugar
3/4 cup dark brown sugar, packed
1 egg, or 2 egg whites
2 tsp. vanilla extract
2 1/2 cups all-purpose flour
1/2 tsp. baking soda
1/8 tsp. salt
1/2 cup miniature semisweet chocolate chips

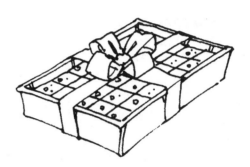

Heat oven to 375°. With an electric mixer, cream butter with sugars. Beat in eggs and vanilla until blended. In another bowl, combine flour, baking soda and salt. Gradually add flour mixture to butter mixture, beating until well blended. Stir in chocolate chips. Press dough into a greased 9 x 13-inch pan and bake for about 10 minutes. Cool in pan and cut into bars.

CLASSIC CHOCOLATE-NUT SQUARES

Makes 16 to 25

These are far better than the purchased variety. For a pretty presentation, place individual squares in fluted paper candy cups.

½ cup butter, softened
½ cup brown sugar, packed
½ tsp. cinnamon
1 egg, separated
½ tsp. vanilla extract

1 cup all-purpose flour
1 cup semisweet chocolate chips, melted
  (see page 4)
⅔ cup coarsely chopped toasted walnuts
  (see page 4)

Heat oven to 350°. Grease a 9-inch square baking pan. With an electric mixer, beat butter, sugar and cinnamon until creamy. Beat in egg yolk and vanilla. Stir in flour just until blended. With lightly greased fingers, press dough evenly in pan. Brush top of dough with lightly beaten egg white. Bake for about 25 minutes, until crust is lightly browned. Cool in pan on a wire rack.

Carefully remove crust from pan and place on a cutting board. With a spatula, spread melted chocolate over crust and sprinkle with walnuts. Place cutting board in the refrigerator until chocolate is firm and squares can be cut without splitting.

CANDIES AND CONFECTIONS

PRESENTING CANDIES AND CONFECTIONS

- Place candies and confections in small fluted paper candy cups. They are available in a wonderful assortment of colors, including prints and metallics.
- Pack candies and confections in useful containers, such as colorful tins, mugs, candy dishes, baking pans, baskets or jewelry boxes. The containers will remain a treasured gift long after the candies have been consumed.
- Personalize containers with your own painted or glued designs (see Packaging Gourmet Gifts, pages 144–151).
- Truffles can be left plain, drizzled with chocolate or rolled in a coating, such as finely chopped nuts, unsweetened cocoa powder, flaked coconut, graham cracker crumbs, cereal crumbs or confectioners' sugar. Place each truffle in a paper candy cup or wrap with colored foil or tissue paper.
- For a glorious gift basket, combine candies and confections with jams, liqueurs, flavored coffees, spiced teas and other goodies.
- Pack a variety of candies and confections in a decorative wrapping or tissue paper-lined candy box. Tie it with a large bow.

CHOCOLATE-PEANUT BUTTER TRUFFLES

Makes about 25

You'll need only about 10 minutes to make these melt-in-your-mouth truffles. Let them set in the refrigerator, place them in pretty candy cups and they're ready to pack. Store truffles for up to 2 weeks in an airtight container in the refrigerator or freeze for up to 4 months. They will thaw in only about 30 minutes.

1 cup peanut butter chips
6 tbs. unsalted butter
1/2 cup unsweetened cocoa powder
1 cup (14 oz. can) sweetened condensed milk
1 tbs. vanilla extract
finely chopped walnuts or sifted unsweetened cocoa powder for coating

Melt peanut butter chips and butter in a heavy saucepan over low heat. Stir in cocoa powder until smooth. Add sweetened condensed milk and cook, stirring, until thickened and mixture pulls away from the bottom of pan, about 4 minutes. Stir in vanilla extract. Cover with plastic wrap and chill in the refrigerator for about 30 minutes, until firm.

Remove mixture from refrigerator and shape into 1-inch balls. Roll balls in nuts or cocoa powder until completely coated. Chill for about 1 hour to blend flavors.

WHITE CHOCOLATE TRUFFLES

Makes about 24

Roll these in finely chopped almonds, or drizzle with chocolate. Store truffles for up to 2 weeks in an airtight container in the refrigerator or freeze for up to 4 months.

1 cup white chocolate chips
$1/4$ cup unsalted butter
$1/2$ cup confectioners sugar, sifted
1 egg yolk
2 tbs. crème de cacao liqueur or vanilla extract
1 cup finely chopped blanched almonds, optional
4 oz. semisweet chocolate chips, melted (see page 4), optional

Melt white chocolate chips with butter in a heavy saucepan over low heat, stirring constantly until blended. Remove from heat and add sugar, egg yolk and liqueur. Beat with an electric mixer until smooth. Cover and refrigerate for 1 hour.

Remove mixture from refrigerator and shape into 1-inch balls. Roll balls in almonds until completely coated. Or, drizzle with melted dark chocolate in a decorative manner. Place chocolate-drizzled truffles on waxed paper for about 30 minutes, until chocolate is set. Cover truffles and refrigerate for at least 8 hours.

PECAN BON BONS

Makes about 24

For a surprise package that is both eye-appealing and palate-pleasing, pack these easy confections with truffles in a box.

$1/4$ cup light corn syrup
1 tsp. vanilla extract
$1/8$ tsp. salt
$1/2$ cup instant nonfat dry milk
$1/4$ cup finely chopped pecans
$1/4$ cup plus 2 tbs. confectioners' sugar

Combine corn syrup, vanilla, salt, dry milk and pecans in a bowl and mix with your hands until well blended. Place mixture on a cutting board. Add $1/4$ cup confectioners' sugar and knead until mixture becomes soft and creamy. Shape into 1-inch balls and dust with 2 tbs. confectioners' sugar. Store in the refrigerator for up to 1 week, or freeze for up to 2 months.

FRUIT-NUT BALLS

A food processor works best to make these all-natural confections. The nuts and fruits should be finely chopped. You can substitute 5 or 6 dried apples or 1 cup dried apricots for pears. You can substitute dried dates or apricots for prunes. The coconut can either be added to the fruit and nut mixture, or the balls can be rolled in coconut to form a coating.

1 cup roasted unsalted soy nuts or sunflower kernels
1/2 cup finely chopped walnuts
5–6 dried pears, finely chopped
1/2 cup raisins, finely chopped
1/2 cup finely chopped pitted prunes
finely grated peel (zest) of 1 orange
1 tbs. orange juice
1 tbs. confectioners' sugar
1/2–1 cup flaked coconut

Combine nuts, dried fruits, orange peel, orange juice and confectioners' sugar in a bowl and mix well. Form mixture into 1-inch balls. Roll balls in coconut until well coated. Store in the refrigerator for up to 1 week.

PEANUT BUTTER AND HONEY BALLS

Makes about 48

Looking for a gift that is easy to prepare? This tops the list and tastes wonderful. Use crunchy or creamy peanut butter. For an elegant presentation, place each ball in a fluted paper candy cup. Pack these in pretty airtight cookie tins and they'll stay fresh in the refrigerator for weeks.

1/2 cup honey
1/2 cup peanut butter
1 cup instant nonfat dry milk
1 cup quick-cooking oats (do not use instant)

In a bowl, mix honey with peanut butter until thoroughly blended. Gradually work in nonfat dry milk and oats. Shape mixture into small balls. Cover and refrigerate.

COCONUT DATE BALLS

Makes about 48

If you're a coconut "nut," use coconut inside and out of these delicacies. Or, you can coat them with finely ground pistachios or other nuts.

1¼ cups sweetened flaked coconut
8 graham crackers
½ lb. (about 1½ cups) pitted dates
¼ cup honey
½ cup finely chopped walnuts
¾ cup finely ground pistachios or other nuts for coating

Heat oven to 350°. Place coconut on an ungreased shallow pan and toast for 3 to 5 minutes, stirring frequently, until golden brown. Cool completely.

Process graham crackers with a food processor to fine crumbs. Add dates and toasted coconut and process until blended. Add honey and process until just combined. Add walnuts and process until mixture holds together. Form mixture into 1-inch balls. Roll balls in ground pistachio nuts until completely coated, pressing slightly to help nuts adhere. Cover and refrigerate.

NUTTY CHOCOLATE TOFFEE

Makes about 2¾ pounds

This delicious toffee is easy to make and easy to store. Spread the toffee quickly in the pan after it is cooked, as it hardens rapidly. Keep toffee refrigerated in an airtight container for up to 2 weeks; freeze for longer storage.

1¼ cups butter
2¼ cups sugar
½ tsp. salt
½ cup water

½ cup chopped hazelnuts
1 cup chopped blanched almonds
1 cup salted pistachio nuts
1½ cups semisweet chocolate chips

Line two 9 x 13-inch pans with foil, crimping the edges over the rim to hold foil in place. Butter foil and set pans aside. In a 5- to 6-quart pot over medium-high heat, cook butter, sugar, salt and water until mixture reaches 250° on a candy thermometer, about 6 to 10 minutes. Stir often. Add hazelnuts and almonds and stir until mixture reaches 300°, about 8 minutes. Remove from heat. Stir in cup of the pistachios and quickly pour mixture into prepared pans; spread evenly with a flexible spatula. Cool for about 2 minutes, until slightly firm. Sprinkle with chocolate chips and let stand for about 5 minutes, until chocolate is softened. Spread softened chocolate over toffee. Chop remaining pistachios and scatter onto soft chocolate. Chill toffee in the refrigerator for about 15 minutes, until chocolate is firm. Remove toffee from pans and break into chunks; remove any foil stuck to toffee.

QUICK MICROWAVE PEANUT BRITTLE
Makes about 1½ cups

Do you like peanut brittle in a hurry? Here's a yummy, quick recipe you can make in your microwave oven. Prepare it in 5 minutes: it is ready in less than 20 minutes.

1 cup sugar
½ cup light corn syrup
1½ cups dry roasted peanuts
1 tbs. butter
1 tsp. vanilla
1 tsp. baking soda

Microwave sugar and corn syrup in large microwave-safe bowl on HIGH for 5 minutes, stirring after 3 minutes. Stir in peanuts. Microwave for an additional 3 to 5 minutes, or until golden brown. Add butter and vanilla; stir until butter is completely melted. Microwave for 1 minute. Stir in baking soda: Mixture will foam. Spread mixture about ¼-inch thick onto a baking sheet. Cool completely. Break into pieces.

PECAN CARAMEL TURTLES

Makes 36

Turtles are delicious and deceptively easy to assemble. Use the individually wrapped caramel candies that you find in the bulk candy section of the supermarket.

108 pecan halves (about 2 cups)
35 vanilla caramels
1½ tbs. margarine or butter

¾ cup semisweet chocolate chips
1–1½ tsp. vegetable oil

Heat oven to 350°. Spread pecans in a single layer in a shallow baking pan and toast for about 10 minutes, stirring occasionally. Line another baking sheet with foil. Arrange pecans in groups of 3, pyramid-fashion, on foil.

In a heavy saucepan, combine caramels and margarine. Heat over low heat and stir gently until melted and smooth. Remove from heat. With a spoon, drop about 1 tsp. melted caramel mixture onto each group of pecans. Let stand for about 20 minutes, until firm.

In a small saucepan, heat chocolate chips with 1 tsp. oil over low heat, stirring constantly, until smooth. Add more oil if necessary to obtain spreading consistency. Remove from heat. With a narrow spatula, spread a small amount of melted chocolate mixture on each pecan cluster. Let stand for about 30 minutes, until chocolate sets and caramel is firm and cool.

CHERRY BRANDY-STUFFED WALNUTS

Makes 24

Kirsch, or kirschwasser, is the German name for cherry brandy. Another flavor of liqueur or brandy can also be used. Pack the stuffed walnuts in a pretty glass candy dish wrapped with colored plastic wrap and top with a perky bow.

1 cup confectioners' sugar
1–2 tbs. kirsch or other liqueur or brandy
48 walnut halves
1/2 cup chocolate chips, melted (see page 4), optional

In a bowl, mix confectioners' sugar and liqueur to form a thick paste. Shape paste into 24 marble-sized balls. Sandwich balls between 2 walnut halves and press together slightly. If desired, dip ends in melted chocolate. Place on waxed paper until chocolate sets.

ROCKY ROAD SNACKS

Makes about 36

These confections are easy to make, but people will think you labored for many hours. They're so simple, the children can help make them! Store in the refrigerator.

2 bars (8 oz. each) milk chocolate, broken into pieces
2½ cups miniature marshmallows
1 cup coarsely chopped nuts

Line an 8-inch square baking pan with foil, extending foil over pan edges. Butter foil and set aside. In a medium saucepan, slowly melt chocolate over low heat, stirring constantly. Remove from heat and stir in marshmallows and nuts. Spread mixture in prepared pan. Chill in the refrigerator for about 1 hour, until firm. Grasp foil edges and lift candy from pan. Place on a cutting board and cut into squares.

CASHEW-MACADAMIA NUT CANDY

Makes about 1½ lb.

This mix is quite sweet and a delicious way to get an energy boost.

2 cups (1½ oz. pkg.) milk chocolate chips
¾ cup coarsely chopped salted or unsalted cashews
¾ cup coarsely chopped salted or unsalted macadamia nuts
½ cup (1 stick) butter, softened
½ cup sugar
2 tbs. light corn syrup

Line a 9-inch square pan with nonstick foil, allowing foil to extend above pan edges. Lightly butter foil and spread bottom with a layer of chocolate chips. In a large, heavy skillet, combine cashews, macadamia nuts, butter, sugar and corn syrup. Cook over low heat, stirring constantly, until butter is melted and sugar is dissolved. Raise heat to medium; cook, stirring constantly, until mixture begins to cling together and turns golden brown. Pour nut mixture over chocolate chips in pan, spreading evenly. Cool. Refrigerate until chocolate is firm. Remove from pan; peel off foil. Break into pieces. Store, tightly covered, in a cool, dry place.

SAVORY SNACKS

PRESENTING SAVORY SNACKS

- Wrap cheese balls with clear or colored plastic wrap. Gather the wrap at the top and tie with a ribbon.
- Package cheeses with a small cutting board and a set of pretty spreading knives.
- Pack cheeses and flavored nut mixes in a picnic basket along with a loaf of French bread or some crackers, sliced meats or patés and a bottle of wine.
- Present nut mixes in a pretty ceramic or glass serving bowl.
- Use a vacuum sealer or locking plastic storage bags to make small parcels of nuts in many different varieties. Affix customized labels describing what's inside. Pack an assortment in a small gift basket.
- Give nut mixes in a decorative jar or storage container. Attach a square of fabric to the top of the jar, if desired, and tie with a pretty ribbon.
- Cut pieces of cardboard and insert in decorative cookie tins as dividers to separate a variety of goodies.
- Package snacks in odd-shaped baskets, such as a cornucopia or fisherman's creel. Line baskets with whole sheets or shreds of colored tissue paper.

CHEESE BALL

Cheese balls make grand gifts because they're pretty, practical and can be stored for a couple of weeks in the refrigerator. They're perfect for appetizers or dessert. Write the following on the gift card: Keep refrigerated; let stand at room temperature for about 30 minutes before serving; serve with crackers or thinly sliced bread.

8 oz. cream cheese, softened
1 oz. blue cheese, crumbled
4 oz. sharp cheddar cheese, grated
2 tbs. white or rosé wine
dash Tabasco Sauce
$1/4$ cup finely chopped toasted almonds (see page 4)

Combine cream cheese, blue cheese and cheddar cheese in a bowl. Add wine and Tabasco and stir until well blended. Refrigerate for at least 3 hours. Remove cheese mixture from bowl and form into a large ball. Roll ball in chopped almonds until completely coated; roll ball lightly on a board to help almonds adhere. Wrap with plastic wrap and refrigerate.

SPICED PECANS CAJUN-STYLE

Makes about 4 cups

You can prepare batches of these ahead of time and keep them on hand for when you need a gift. They're perfect for appetizers or snacks. Store in airtight containers or plastic baggies.

4 tbs. unsalted butter
1 lb. pecan halves
1/2 cup light brown sugar
1 tsp. paprika
1 tsp. dried basil
1 tsp. dried oregano

1 tsp. dried thyme
2 tsp. chili powder
1 tbs. ground cumin
1/4 cup cider vinegar
salt to taste

Heat oven to 325°. Melt butter over medium heat in a large skillet. Add pecans and sauté until lightly browned, about 3 minutes. Add brown sugar and cook until caramelized. Stir in paprika, basil, oregano, thyme, chili powder and cumin. Add vinegar and cook over medium heat until all the liquid has evaporated. Season with salt. Spread pecans on a cookie sheet and bake until crisp, about 3 to 5 minutes.

GOAT CHEESE LOGS

Makes three 8-ounce logs

Shape goat cheese into 3 cylinders and roll each in a different coating: finely ground almonds; chopped fresh parsley; and cranberries mixed with walnuts. Wrap each log separately. Along with the cheese, give a box of elegant crackers or Italian bread for serving.

1½ lb. soft goat cheese, room temperature
2 tsp. extra virgin olive oil
2 tsp. dried thyme
2 oil-packed sun-dried tomatoes, drained, coarsely chopped

COATINGS
½ cup coarsely chopped almonds
½ cup coarsely chopped fresh parsley
¼ cup coarsely chopped walnuts mixed with ¼ cup coarsely chopped fresh cranberries

In a food processor, combine cheese, oil, thyme and tomatoes and process until well blended. Divide mixture into thirds and shape each third into a cylinder. Place coatings in each of 3 shallow bowls. Roll each cylinder in a different coating until completely covered; roll cylinders lightly on a board to help coatings adhere. Wrap with plastic wrap and refrigerate.

BARBECUE-FLAVORED PEANUTS

Makes 3 cups

Add your favorite barbecue sauce to peanuts for scrumptious flavor.

$1/3$ cup mesquite or other smoke-flavored
   barbecue sauce

$1/2$ tsp. onion salt
3 cups unsalted dry-roasted peanuts

Heat oven to 300°. Mix all ingredients in a large bowl until nuts are well coated. Spread coated nuts on a lightly greased baking sheet. Bake for 20 minutes, stirring after 10 minutes. Cool completely.

CURRIED PEANUTS

Makes 2 cups

This combination uses a classic East Indian flavoring.

2 cups roasted, salted, blanched peanuts
2 tsp. curry powder

1 tsp. seasoned salt
$1/2$ tsp. garlic powder

Heat oven to 350°. Combine ingredients in a bowl and mix until nuts are well coated. Spread on an ungreased baking sheet and bake for about 5 minutes. Cool completely.

PERKY PECANS

You'll tip your ten-gallon hat to this southwestern treat that's flavored with chili powder, cumin and cayenne pepper.

⅓ cup butter or margarine
2 tbs. Worcestershire sauce
1½ tsp. garlic salt
½ tsp. ground cumin
½ tsp. chili powder
⅛ tsp. cayenne pepper
3 cups pecan halves
2 tbs. coarse salt

Heat oven to 325°. Melt butter over medium-low heat in a large saucepan. Add Worcestershire sauce, garlic salt, cumin, chili powder and cayenne pepper and simmer over low heat for 5 minutes. Add nuts and stir to coat. Spread nuts in a single layer on a baking sheet and bake for 15 to 20 minutes, stirring after 10 minutes. Remove from oven and sprinkle with coarse salt. Cool completely.

SWEDISH NUTS

Makes about 3$\frac{1}{2}$ cups

These marvelous meringue-covered nuts require a little extra preparation, but they are well worth it.

1$\frac{1}{2}$ cups blanched almonds or pecans
2 cups walnut halves
2 egg whites
1 cup sugar
dash salt
$\frac{1}{2}$ cup butter or margarine

Heat oven to 325°. Place almonds and walnuts in a single layer on a baking sheet and toast for about 5 minutes, until almonds are light brown. Cool. In a medium bowl, beat egg whites with sugar and salt until stiff peaks form. Fold in nuts. Melt butter on a large, rimmed baking sheet in oven. Spread nut mixture over butter. Bake for about 30 minutes, stirring every 10 minutes, until butter is absorbed. Cool.

SPICY MIXED NUTS

Here's the ideal snack gift to bring a host or hostess for a football party. They'll warm you through if you're nibbling from a stadium seat, too.

1 tsp. garlic salt
1/2 tsp. ground cumin
1/2 tsp. chili powder
1/2 tsp. curry powder
1/2 tsp. cayenne pepper

1/4 tsp. ground ginger
1/4 tsp. cinnamon
2 tbs. peanut oil
2 cups mixed raw nuts
coarse salt to taste

Heat oven to 325°. Mix garlic salt, cumin, chili powder, curry, cayenne, ginger and cinnamon in a small bowl. Heat oil in a skillet over low heat. Add spice mixture and cook, stirring, for 3 to 4 minutes. Remove from heat, add nuts and stir until nuts are well coated. Transfer nuts to a baking sheet and spread in single layer. Bake for 15 minutes, tossing with a spatula every 5 minutes. Sprinkle with coarse salt and cool.

NUT AND CEREAL PARTY MIX

Makes about 10 cups

Use 2⅓ cups each of three favorite cereals, such as Chex, Cherrios and Puffed Rice. Store in airtight containers.

6 tbs. margarine or butter
2 tbs. Worcestershire sauce
1½ tsp. seasoned salt
½ tsp. garlic powder
½ tsp. onion powder

7 cups dry cereal
1 cup mixed nuts
1 cup miniature pretzels
1 cup bite-sized bagel chips

To make in the oven, heat oven to 250°. Melt margarine in a roasting pan in oven. Stir in Worcestershire sauce, seasoned salt, garlic powder and onion powder. Add remaining ingredients and stir until well coated. Bake for 1 hour, stirring every 15 minutes. Spread on paper towels to cool.

To make in the microwave, melt margarine in a large microwave-safe bowl. Stir in Worcestershire sauce, seasoned salt, garlic powder and onion powder. Add remaining ingredients and stir until well coated. Cook on HIGH for 5 to 6 minutes, stirring with a rubber spatula every 2 minutes and scraping the sides of bowl. Spread on paper towels to cool.

QUICK BREADS AND YEAST BREADS

PRESENTING QUICK BREADS AND YEAST BREADS

- Quick breads stay fresh for days if they are well wrapped with foil and refrigerated or frozen. Keep a few loaves on hand for emergency gifts.
- Bake breads in disposable foil pans. After cooling, return bread to pan and wrap for an interesting presentation.
- For a special gift, bake bread in a good-quality nonstick loaf pan. Give the pan with the bread as a gift along with a slicing knife and a flavored butter or spread.
- For soft breads, remove the bread from the pan and place on a foil-lined piece of cardboard that is a little larger than the loaf. Wrap the bread and the cardboard with plastic wrap and tie with a broad ribbon and wide bow. Attach a card with the name of the bread.
- Firm breads can be wrapped in parchment or brown paper without a rigid base. Decorate the brown paper with vegetable or herb imprints (see pages 147 and 148) if desired. Tie with raffia and an herb sprig for a natural look.
- Breads make excellent additions to gift baskets. Assemble them according to a theme, and include complementary accompaniments, such as flavored butters, jams or spreads.

PINEAPPLE-ZUCCHINI QUICK BREAD

Makes 2 loaves

For a fruitier bread, you can replace half of the nuts with dried currants.

3 eggs
1 cup oil or baking fat substitute (see page 6)
2 cups sugar
2 tsp. vanilla extract
2 cups coarsely shredded zucchini
1 can (8 oz.) crushed pineapple, well drained
3 cups all-purpose flour

2 tsp. baking soda
$\frac{1}{2}$ tsp. baking powder
$\frac{1}{2}$ tsp. salt
$1\frac{1}{2}$ tsp. cinnamon
$\frac{3}{4}$ tsp. nutmeg
1 cup finely chopped nuts

Heat oven to 350°. Grease and flour two 9 x 5 x 3-inch loaf pans. In a large bowl, beat eggs lightly with an electric mixer. Add oil, sugar and vanilla and beat until thick and foamy. Stir in zucchini and pineapple with a spoon. In another bowl, combine flour, baking soda, baking powder, salt, cinnamon, nutmeg and nuts. Stir flour mixture into zucchini mixture until just blended. Divide batter equally between pans. Bake for about 1 hour, until a wooden pick inserted in the center comes out clean. Cool bread in pans for 10 minutes. Transfer loaves to wire racks to cool completely. Wrap cooled bread with foil and store in the refrigerator for up to 1 week or in the freezer for up to 2 months.

LEMON POUND CAKE WITHOUT THE POUNDS

Here's a guilt-free, sour cream-based pound cake with several alternative flavorings. Cake flour, made from soft wheat, contributes to a light texture. If you don't have cake flour, try the following substitution: for each cup of cake flour, measure 1 cup less 2 tbs. all-purpose flour; sift just before using. Be sure to use a margarine that's suitable for baking.

2½ cups sugar
¾ cup margarine
5-6 egg whites, or 1⅓ cups egg substitute
1½ cups low-fat sour cream
1 tsp. baking soda

4½ cups cake flour
¼ tsp. salt
¼ tsp. nutmeg
1 tsp. vanilla extract
1 tsp. lemon extract

Heat oven to 325°. Spray a 10-inch tube or Bundt pan with nonstick cooking spray. In a large bowl, cream sugar and margarine with an electric mixer. Gradually add egg whites one at a time and blend well. In another bowl, combine sour cream and baking soda; stir well. In another bowl, mix flour with salt and nutmeg. Add flour mixture to margarine mixture alternately with sour cream mixture while mixing at low speed; begin and end with flour mixture. Stir in extracts. Spoon batter into prepared pan.

Bake cake for 1 hour and 35 minutes, or until a wooden pick inserted in the center of cake comes out clean. Cool in pan for 10 minutes. Transfer cake to a wire rack to cool completely. Wrap cooled cake with foil and store in the refrigerator for up to 1 week.

VARIATIONS

COCONUT POUND CAKE: Substitute 1 tsp. coconut extract for lemon extract.
ALMOND POUND CAKE: Substitute 1 tsp. almond extract for lemon extract.
RUM POUND CAKE: Substitute 1 tsp. rum extract for lemon extract.
CHOCOLATE MARBLE POUND CAKE: Increase vanilla extract to 2 tsp. and omit lemon extract. Transfer $1/3$ of the batter to a bowl and stir in $1/4$ cup cocoa powder until blended. Spoon $1/2$ of the remaining light batter into baking pan; top with chocolate batter and follow with remaining light batter. Using a knife, cut through batter to make a marbled pattern.

BANANA-RAISIN-RUM QUICK BREAD

Makes 1 loaf

Rum-soaked raisins make this variation of banana bread unique. Soak raisins in rum for several hours and drain before assembling the recipe. You will need 3 to 4 medium-sized bananas.

1 cup sugar
1 cup margarine or softened butter
2 eggs
1½ cups mashed ripe bananas
⅓ cup water
1⅔ cups all-purpose flour

1 tsp. baking soda
¼ tsp. baking powder
½ tsp. salt
½ cup chopped almonds or walnuts
½ cup golden raisins soaked in ¼ cup rum
  or brandy

Heat oven to 350°. Grease the bottom of a 9 x 5 x 3-inch loaf pan. In a large bowl, cream sugar and margarine with an electric mixer. Stir in eggs until blended. Add mashed bananas and water and beat for 30 seconds. In another bowl, mix flour, baking soda, baking powder and salt; add to banana mixture and stir until just moistened. Stir in nuts and raisins. Pour batter into pan and bake for about 1 hour, until a wooden pick inserted in the center comes out clean. Cool bread in pan for 5 minutes. Transfer to a wire rack to cool completely. Wrap cooled bread with foil and store in the refrigerator for up to 1 week or in the freezer for up to 2 months.

ORANGE QUICK BREAD

Makes 1 loaf

Orange flavor permeates this bread when the orange glaze seeps through the holes that are poked into the warm loaf. Try it with lemon, too.

1¾ cups all-purpose flour
1 cup sugar
1 tsp. baking powder
½ tsp. salt
2 eggs
½ cup milk

½ cup vegetable oil
1 tbs. grated fresh orange peel (zest)

GLAZE
2 tbs. orange juice
1 cup confectioners' sugar

Heat oven to 350°. Grease a 9 x5 x 3-inch loaf pan. In a large bowl, combine flour, sugar, baking powder and salt. In a small bowl, beat eggs; stir in milk, oil and orange peel. Add egg mixture to flour mixture and stir until just combined. Pour batter into prepared pan. Bake for 40 to 45 minutes, until a wooden pick inserted in the center comes out clean. Mix together Glaze ingredients until smooth. Remove bread from oven. With a wooden skewer, poke about 16 holes into bread all the way to the bottom of pan. Drizzle glaze over warm bread and into holes. Cool bread in pan for 5 minutes; remove bread from pan and place on a rack to cool completely. Wrap cooled bread with foil and store in the refrigerator for up to 1 week or in the freezer for up to 2 months.

PUMPKIN QUICK BREAD

Makes 2 loaves

This recipe features raisins or dates, but you can substitute walnuts or your favorite dried fruits. Store bread in the refrigerator.

3 cups all-purpose flour
1 tsp. salt
2 cups sugar
2 tsp. baking soda
2 cups (29 oz. can) pumpkin puree
1 cup canola or other vegetable oil

4 eggs, beaten
1/2 cup water
1 tsp. cinnamon
1 tsp. nutmeg
1/2 tsp. ground ginger or cloves
1 cup raisins or chopped dates

Heat oven to 350°. Lightly grease two 9 x 5 x 3-inch loaf pans with nonstick cooking spray. In a small bowl, combine flour, salt, sugar and baking soda. In a large bowl, mix pumpkin, oil, eggs, water and spices with a wire whisk until well blended. Add flour mixture and stir until ingredients are just mixed, taking care not to overmix. Stir in raisins. Pour batter evenly in prepared pans. Bake for 50 to 60 minutes, until a wooden pick inserted in the center comes out clean. Remove bread from pans and transfer to a wire rack to cool completely. Wrap cooled bread with foil and store in the refrigerator for up to 1 week or in the freezer for up to 2 months.

HOW TO MAKE YEAST BREADS

To make yeast breads with a bread machine, add ingredients to the bread machine pan according to manufacturer's instructions. Set on the dough cycle; then, shape and bake dough according to the recipe. Or, bake in the bread machine according to the recipe.

To make yeast breads with a food processor or heavy-duty mixer, warm water or milk to 110° to 115° and make sure other ingredients are at room temperature. Combine all dry ingredients, including yeast, in the workbowl or mixer bowl and process for 10 seconds. With the machine running, pour remaining dough ingredients into the machine until the dough forms a ball. Process dough ball for about 1 minute with a food processor or 5 minutes with a mixer. Or, knead by hand for about 5 to 10 minutes. Knead in additions. Shape dough into a ball, place in a greased bowl and cover with a kitchen towel. Place in a warm, draft-free location until dough has doubled in size. Shape and bake dough according to the recipe.

While mixing, yeast dough should come together in a smooth ball that is not too sticky. If the dough is too dry, add 1 tbs. water at a time until it reaches the proper consistency; if it is too wet, add 1 tbs. flour.

CRANBERRY-ORANGE BREAD

Makes 1 loaf

Use whole cranberries in season or dried cranberries the rest of the year for this bread. You can also use homemade or canned whole-berry cranberry sauce to replace some of the liquid. Additional whole cranberries or craisins can be kneaded in if desired.

DOUGH
1/8 cup water
1/4 cup frozen orange juice concentrate,
   thawed
3/4 cup whole-berry cranberry sauce
1/2 tsp. finely grated orange peel (zest)
1 tbs. butter or margarine
1 tbs. brown sugar

1 tsp. salt
2 3/4 cups bread flour
5/8 cup whole wheat flour
2 tsp. fast-acting yeast

ADDITIONS
1/4 cup whole fresh or dried cranberries
1/4 cup raisins

Make dough according to desired method on page 67. To bake in the bread machine, set cycle to raisin and set crust color to medium. To bake in the oven, heat oven to 375°. Punch down dough after first rise. Shape dough into a rectangle and fold into thirds to fit a greased 9 x 5 x 3-inch loaf pan. Let dough rise for about 45 to 60 minutes, until doubled in size. Bake for 25 to 30 minutes, until lightly browned on top and bread sounds hollow when thumped.

ORANGE POPPY SEED BREAD

Makes 1 loaf

Make this never-fail recipe with either sour cream or plain low-fat yogurt.

$1/4$ cup water
$1/2$ cup sour cream or plain low-fat yogurt
$1/4$ cup frozen orange juice concentrate, thawed
2 tbs. butter or margarine, cut into pieces
1 egg

4 tsp. sugar
$1/4$ cup poppy seeds
1 tsp. salt
$2^3/4$ cups bread flour
$5/8$ cup whole wheat flour
2 tsp. fast-acting yeast

Make dough according to desired method on page 67. To bake in the bread machine, set cycle to basic or white and set crust color to medium. To bake in the oven, heat oven to 375°. Punch down dough after first rise. Shape dough into a rectangle and fold into thirds to fit a greased 9 x 5 x 3-inch loaf pan. Let dough rise for about 45 to 60 minutes, until doubled in size. Bake for 25 to 30 minutes, until lightly browned on top and bread sounds hollow when thumped.

SALSA BREAD

Makes 1 loaf

This bread has a wonderful color, texture and flavor. Use a mild tomato salsa. You can vary the flavor in an infinite number of ways by using a fruit-flavored or other type of salsa.

3/4 cup salsa

1/3 cup plus 1 tbs. water

2 tbs. softened butter or margarine

2 tbs. sugar

1 tsp. salt

2 tbs. chopped fresh cilantro

2 tbs. chopped fresh tarragon

3 cups bread flour

2 tsp. fast-acting yeast

Make dough according to desired method on page 67. To bake in the bread machine, set cycle to basic or white and set crust color to light or medium. To bake in the oven, heat oven to 375°. Punch down dough after first rise. Shape dough into a rectangle and fold into thirds to fit a greased 9 x 5 x 3-inch loaf pan. Let dough rise for about 45 to 60 minutes, until doubled in size. Bake for 25 to 30 minutes, until lightly browned on top and bread sounds hollow when thumped.

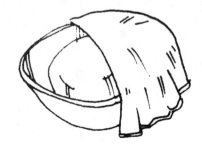

BLACK OLIVE RYE BREAD

The olives give this bread great texture, color and flavor. Look for vital gluten in health or specialty food stores. It's usually sold in bulk. If your bread machine does not have a beep, add the second addition of olives at the beginning of the second kneading period. You can also shape this bread into a round and bake it on parchment.

DOUGH

3/4 cup water
5/8 cup milk
1 1/2 tbs. softened butter or margarine
3 tbs. molasses
1 tbs. sliced black olives
1 tbs. caraway seeds
1 1/2 tsp. salt

1 1/2 cups whole wheat flour
1 1/2 cups bread flour
1 cup rye flour
3 tbs. vital gluten
2 tsp. fast-acting yeast

ADDITIONS

1/3 cup sliced black olives, patted dry

Make dough according to desired method on page 67. To bake in the bread machine, set cycle to raisin and set crust color to medium. To bake in the oven, heat oven to 400°. Punch down dough after first rise. Shape dough into a rectangle and fold into thirds to fit a greased 9 x 5 x 3-inch loaf pan. Let dough rise for about 45 to 60 minutes, until doubled in size. Bake for 25 to 30 minutes, until lightly browned on top and bread sounds hollow when thumped.

ANIMAL-SHAPED BREAD

This is a wonderful gift to make with children. Start with these designs; then, create some of your own. Use the drawings in children's books for inspiration. You can simulate an animal or other shape with just a few cuts with a sharp knife. For facial details, use nuts, raisins, other dried fruits and sesame and/or caraway seeds.

DOUGH

1/2 cup water
1 egg yolk, beaten
2 tbs. butter, softened
1/4 cup sugar
1 tsp. salt
3 cups bread flour
1/4 cup whole wheat flour
2 tsp. fast-acting yeast

DECORATIONS

1 egg white beaten with 1 tsp. water
nuts, dried fruits and/or seeds

Make dough according to desired method on page 67. If making in a bread machine, set it on the dough cycle. Divide dough into eight to ten 3-inch balls. Form and decorate desired animal shapes using diagrams, or make up your own. Use egg white to help decorations adhere. Place decorated animal shapes on a greased baking sheet and spray lightly with water. Cover with oiled plastic wrap and let rise until doubled in size, about 20 minutes. Heat oven to 375°. Brush shapes with beaten egg white mixture and bake for 10 to 12 minutes, until lightly browned.

RABBIT-SHAPED BREAD

Shape 1 dough ball into a flattened oval, about ½-inch thick, on a bread board. With a sharp knife, make a long slice at the top for the "ear" and make 2 slices for the "legs" at the bottom rear, as shown. Add a raisin for the "eye."

BEAR-SHAPED BREAD

Shape a dough ball into a flattened oval, about ½-inch thick, on a bread board. With a sharp knife, make 6 angled cuts as shown. Remove dough between cuts 5 and 6. Divide removed dough into 2 pieces and attach at the top front of the bear's "head" as shown to resemble "ears." Pull out and elongate the "nose" and "tail" respectively. Add a raisin for the "eye."

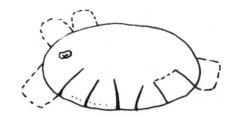

SWEET AND SAVORY TOPPINGS AND SPREADS

PRESENTING TOPPINGS AND SPREADS

- Cover the tops of jars with squares of brightly colored fabric. Cut a circle from printed light cotton fabric that is about 1½ inches larger than the jar top. Use pinking shears to make a decorative edge. Place the fabric square on top of the covered jar and secure with a ribbon, length of raffia, yarn or other decorative tie just under the lid. Attach a tag with the name of the item and storage information.

- Cover the bottoms of jars by placing them in the center of a large square of pretty fabric. Bring the edges up around the jar and tie a ribbon securely just below the top of the jar so the edges of the fabric flare outwards. Trim if necessary.

- Affix decorative adhesive labels on jars or bottles with the ingredients and storage requirements.

- Place an assortment of complementary toppings and spreads in a gift basket. Be sure to label each one clearly. Offer serving suggestions on the gift enclosure.

- Pack flavored jams, fruit butters, fruit curds, honeys or flavored dairy butters along with a loaf of quick bread in a lovely basket. Include a sachet of spiced tea, coffee or hot cocoa mix for a truly special gift.

- For a double-duty gift, package jars of homemade mustards with a recipe that uses mustard.

QUICK STRAWBERRY JAM

Makes one 6-ounce jar

It's easy to make an individual recipe of jam in about 5 minutes in the microwave. Store opened jars of jam in the refrigerator for up to 2 months.

½ pt. (6-8 oz.) ripe strawberries, hulled
¼ tsp. freshly grated lemon peel (zest)
2 tsp. fresh lemon juice

2 tsp. powdered fruit pectin
½ cup sugar

Mash berries with a blender or fork and place in a 2-quart glass bowl with lemon peel and juice. Stir in pectin until well blended. Place bowl in the microwave and cook uncovered on HIGH for about 2 minutes, until mixture reaches a full rolling boil around the edges. Rotate bowl ½ turn after 1 minute. Stir in sugar until completely dissolved. Cook uncovered on HIGH for 1 to 2 minutes, until mixture returns to rolling boil. When boiling, cook on HIGH for 1½ minutes. Remove mixture from microwave and let stand for about 1 minute. With a metal spoon, skim and discard any foam on the surface of mixture; stir mixture well. Pour mixture into a sterilized 6-ounce canning jar (see page 6). Wipe the rim with a clean cloth. Seal immediately (see page 6). Let jam stand on the counter until cool. Refrigerate for 24 hours or until jam sets softly before using.

VARIATION: QUICK APRICOT JAM

Substitute 2 to 3 peeled and chopped ripe apricots (about 6 to 8 oz.) for strawberries.

VARIATION: QUICK MANGO JAM

Substitute $1/2$ large, peeled, chopped, firm ripe mango (about 8 oz.) for strawberries. Substitute lime peel and lime juice for lemon peel and lemon juice. Decrease pectin to $1 1/4$ tsp.

LARGE RECIPE QUICK BLUEBERRY JAM   Makes three 6-ounce jars

If you have an abundance of fruit, do not double the recipe. Instead, make separate batches. Or, freeze measured amounts of fruit with sugar and lemon juice. They can be thawed and made into fresh jam any time.

3 cups blueberries, slightly crushed to yield
  2 cups
1½ cups sugar
½ tsp. butter or margarine

¼ cup lemon juice
½ tsp. grated fresh lemon peel (zest)
¼ tsp. cinnamon

Place blueberries in a 3-quart glass bowl. Add remaining ingredients and let stand for about 30 minutes, until juices are released. If necessary, crush fruit slightly with a fork to release more juice.

Microwave mixture uncovered on HIGH for 6 to 8 minutes, until mixture starts to boil. Stir. Cook on HIGH for about 6 minutes, stirring every 2 minutes. Spoon 1 tbs. jam mixture into a custard cup; cool in the freezer for about 5 minutes and check consistency. For a thicker jam, reheat mixture to boiling, boil for 2 additional minutes. Retest for consistency.

Remove mixture from microwave and let stand for about 10 minutes. With a metal spoon, skim and discard any foam on the surface of mixture; stir mixture well. Pour mixture into 3 hot sterilized 6-ounce canning jars (see page 6). Wipe jar rims with a clean cloth. Seal immediately (see page 6). Let jam stand on the counter until cool. Refrigerate for 2 to 3 hours or until jam sets softly before using.

VARIATIONS

LARGE RECIPE QUICK PEACH OR NECTARINE JAM: Substitute 2 cups peeled, chopped ripe peaches or nectarines for blueberries. Reduce lemon juice to 1 tbs. and omit lemon zest and cinnamon. Stir in 2 drops almond extract after cooking.

LARGE RECIPE QUICK PLUM JAM: Substitute 2 cups peeled chopped purple plums for blueberries. Reduce lemon juice to 1 tbs. and omit lemon zest and cinnamon.

LARGE RECIPE QUICK SWEET CHERRY JAM: Substitute 2 cups pitted chopped cherries for blueberries. Increase lemon peel to 1 tsp. and increase cinnamon to $1/2$ tsp.

BANANA JAM

Makes four 1-quart jars

Since bananas are always in season, you can whip up a batch of banana jam whenever the mood strikes. Or, store jars of it on the shelf, ready for gift-giving. This recipe can be halved or quartered if desired.

12 cups sliced, medium-ripe bananas
6 cups sugar
1½ cups orange juice
¾ cup lemon or lime juice

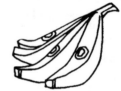

Cook all ingredients in a 6-quart nonaluminum saucepan over medium heat until sugar is dissolved. Reduce heat to low and simmer for about 15 minutes, until mixture thickens. Pour into hot sterilized 16-ounce canning jars and seal immediately, following instructions on page 6. Let jam stand on the counter until cool. Refrigerate after opening.

JALAPEÑO JELLY

Makes eight 6-ounce jars

This jelly is perfect to serve as a condiment for poultry dishes. It's also delicious on its own or with cream cheese spread on crackers. Remember to remove the seeds and ribs of the peppers before chopping.

1½ cups finely chopped green bell peppers
1 cup finely chopped jalapeño peppers
6½ cups sugar
1½ cups cider vinegar
1 bottle (6 oz.) liquid fruit pectin
¼ tsp. green food coloring, optional

Mix bell peppers, jalapeño peppers, sugar and vinegar in a 6-quart nonaluminum saucepan and bring to a rolling boil over high heat. Add liquid fruit pectin and return to rolling boil, stirring constantly for 1 minute. Remove from heat and let stand for 1 to 2 minutes. Skim foam and discard. Stir in food coloring if desired. Pour mixture through a strainer into hot sterilized 6-ounce canning jars and seal immediately, following instructions on page 6. Let jam stand on the counter until cool. Refrigerate after opening.

SPICED PEACH PRESERVES

Makes six 8-ounce jars

Make this recipe when peaches are in season and save for giving as gifts later in the year. To peel peaches easily, dip them quickly into very hot water.

5 cups sugar
1/2 cup cider vinegar or lemon juice
1 tsp. cinnamon

1 tsp. ground cloves
1 tsp. ground allspice
6 lb. firm, ripe peaches, peeled, thinly sliced

Mix all ingredients in a large bowl and let stand for about 1 hour until juices are released. In a heavy 8- to 10-quart nonaluminum saucepan, bring mixture to a boil over high heat and stir just until sugar dissolves. Pour mixture through a colander, catching the juice in a bowl. Set peaches aside. Measure 6 cups juice, adding water if necessary, and heat over medium-high heat until reduced by half, about 8 to 10 minutes. Add peach slices and cook over medium heat for about 25 minutes, stirring often, until preserves are golden and thick. Skim foam and discard. Ladle hot preserves into 6 hot sterilized 8-ounce canning jars and seal immediately, following instructions on page 6. Let preserves stand on the counter until cool. Refrigerate after opening.

APPLE BUTTER

Sauce-like fruit butters are so good, they are usually eaten before they can spoil.

3½ cups apple cider
4 cups water
8 large Golden Delicious or other apples peeled, cored, sliced
1½ cups sugar
1 tsp. salt
½ tsp. cinnamon
1 stick cinnamon
1 tsp. nutmeg

In a 4-quart heavy nonaluminum saucepan, combine cider and water. Bring to a boil over medium-high heat; add apples and reduce heat to low. Simmer uncovered for 45 minutes, stirring occasionally. Stir in sugar, salt, cinnamon and nutmeg and stir until well blended. Cook uncovered over low heat, stirring occasionally, for 20 to 25 minutes, until mixture thickens to the consistency of hot applesauce. Remove and discard cinnamon stick. Ladle into sterilized canning jars and seal immediately, following instructions on page 6. Refrigerate after opening and use within 2 weeks.

CHERRY-PINEAPPLE BUTTER

Makes six 8-ounce jars

This combination is wonderful when fresh cherries are in season, but it can be made with canned cherries, too.

8 cups fresh or canned pitted cherries
1 cup water
1 cup canned crushed pineapple
2 tbs. lemon juice
4 cups sugar

Combine all ingredients in a heavy 6- to 8-quart nonaluminum saucepan. Bring to a boil over high heat, reduce heat to low and simmer, stirring frequently, until thickened, about 30 minutes. Ladle into sterilized 8-ounce canning jars and seal immediately, following instructions on page 6. Refrigerate after opening and use within 2 weeks.

SPICED PUMPKIN BUTTER

Makes five 6-ounce jars

Since canned pumpkin is available all year, you can make this tasty spread anytime. This can be stored for several months.

1 can (16 oz.) solid-pack pumpkin
1/3 cup brown sugar, packed
1/4 cup honey
2 tsp. lemon juice
1/2 tsp. ground allspice
1/4 tsp. ground ginger
1/4 tsp. cinnamon
1/8 tsp. ground cloves

In a heavy 4-quart nonaluminum saucepan, combine pumpkin, brown sugar, honey, lemon juice, allspice, ginger, cinnamon and cloves. Bring to a boil over medium-high heat, stirring frequently. Reduce heat to low and simmer, stirring occasionally, for about 20 minutes, until thickened. Ladle into sterilized 6-ounce canning jars and seal immediately, following instructions on page 6. Refrigerate after opening and use within 2 weeks.

RASPBERRY-MINT HONEY

Makes four 8-ounce jars

You can substitute other types of chopped seasonal fruits and herbs in this easy recipe. To check the honey's consistency, put 1 tbs. on a plate and cool. If it needs to be thicker, simmer for 3 to 5 minutes. Honey is ready for gift-giving as soon as it is cooled and poured into jars.

4 cups mild-flavored honey, such as clover or orange blossom
2 cups frozen raspberries
1/3 cup chopped fresh mint leaves

Place ingredients in a heavy 4-quart nonaluminum saucepan and heat over medium-high heat, stirring occasionally, until simmering. Reduce heat to low and simmer for about 20 minutes. Cool completely. Pour mixture through a fine strainer into sterilized jars (see page 6) and tighten lids. Store flavored honey at room temperature for up to 4 weeks. For longer storage, seal jars according to instructions on page 6.

GRAPEFRUIT-HONEY MARMALADE

Makes four 8-ounce jars

Be sure to wash the grapefruits carefully and use only the colored part of the peel, as the white pith is extremely bitter. Use Ruby Red, Texas Flame or Florida grapefruits.

4 cups mild-flavored honey, such as clover or orange blossom
finely chopped peel (zest) of 3-4 grapefruits

Combine ingredients in a heavy 4-quart nonaluminum saucepan. Heat over medium-high heat, stirring occasionally, until simmering. Reduce heat to low and simmer for about 10 minutes. Cool completely. Pour into sterilized jars (see page 6) and tighten lids. Store at room temperature for up to 4 weeks. For longer storage, seal according to instructions on page 6.

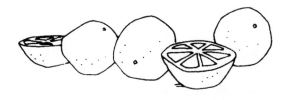

LEMON CURD

Fruit curd is an English delicacy. It should be refrigerated as soon as it cools. This recipe will keep refrigerated for 1 month. If you don't have a double boiler, use a heatproof bowl set over a pan of simmering water.

juice and finely sliced peel (zest) of 3 lemons 1 cup sugar
3/4 cup unsalted butter 4 eggs, beaten

Combine all ingredients in the top of a double boiler. Cook gently over simmering water, stirring until sugar is dissolved. Strain mixture through a medium mesh strainer and discard lemon peel. Return mixture to double boiler and cook over simmering water for about 45 minutes, stirring frequently, until thickened. Pour into small jars, cool completely, secure lid on jar to form an airtight seal and refrigerate.

VARIATION: MICROWAVE LEMON CURD

Blend grated peel (zest) and juice from 3 lemons, 1 cup sugar and 3 eggs in a microwave-safe bowl with a wire whisk. Slowly whisk 1/2 cup hot melted unsalted butter into juice mixture. Cook on HIGH for 3 to 4 minutes until thickened, whisking well after each minute. Pour into small jars, cool, seal and refrigerate.

ORANGE CURD

Makes two 8-ounce jars

Orange curd has a distinct and delectable flavor. You can double the recipe if desired. Use a heatproof bowl set over a pan of simmering water if you don't have a double boiler.

3 eggs
2 egg yolks
1 cup sugar
1/2 cup freshly squeezed orange juice
grated peel (zest) from 1 large orange
1/4 cup butter, cut into pieces

Combine eggs, egg yolks and sugar in a medium bowl and beat with a wire whisk until smooth. Mix in orange juice and peel. Place mixture in the top of a double boiler and cook, stirring vigorously with a wooden spoon, until mixture thickens. Remove curd from heat and stir in butter until melted and well blended. Pour into small jars, cool completely, secure lid on jar to form an airtight seal and refrigerate.

CRANBERRY-SAGE MUSTARD

Makes one 8-ounce jar

The flavor of this mustard is so good, make a double or triple batch and keep some for yourself.

1 jar (7½ oz.) Dijon mustard
1 tbs. mustard seeds

1 tbs. chopped dried cranberries
1 tbs. chopped fresh sage leaves

Blend all ingredients with a food processor or blender. Transfer to a sterilized glass or ceramic jar (see page 6) and cover securely. Store in the refrigerator for up to 6 months.

HORSERADISH MUSTARD

Makes one 8-ounce jar

Thin this down with vinegar and use as a fat-free salad dressing.

⅔ cup honey
⅓ cup Dijon mustard

2 tbs. prepared white horseradish

Combine all ingredients in a bowl and mix until well blended. Transfer to a sterilized glass or ceramic jar (see page 6) and cover securely. Store in the refrigerator for up to 6 months.

HERBED HONEY MUSTARD

Makes one 8-ounce jar

Dry mustard and mustard seeds provide a solid foundation for this tangy relish.

1/2 cup honey
1/3 cup mustard seeds
1/3 cup distilled white vinegar
1/4 cup dry mustard

1/2 tsp. dried thyme
1/2 tsp. dried tarragon
1/4 tsp. garlic powder

Process all ingredients with a blender for about 2 minutes, until seeds are ground. Transfer to a sterilized glass or ceramic jar (see page 6) and cover securely. Store in the refrigerator for 2 weeks before using. Use within 6 months.

TARRAGON MUSTARD

Makes one 8-ounce jar

Use your favorite Dijon for a combination that is delicious with fish and poultry dishes.

1 cup fresh tarragon leaves
1/2 cup finely minced shallots

4 cups Dijon mustard
1 tbs. dry vermouth or white wine

Finely chop tarragon leaves. In a bowl, mix tarragon, shallots, mustard and vermouth with a wire whisk until blended. Pour into a sterilized glass or ceramic jar (see page 6). Cover securely and store in the refrigerator for up to 1 month.

FLAVORED DAIRY BUTTERS

Flavored dairy butters should be refrigerated immediately after making and can be stored tightly wrapped in the refrigerator for up to 2 weeks. They can also be frozen for up to 2 months. Margarine can be used in place of butter, but lower fat varieties do not hold a shape well. Create a design on the top of the butter with some of the ingredients that you used. Sprigs of fresh herbs or nut pieces work well. See page 4 for information on toasting nuts, melting chocolate and softening butter.

With a wire whisk, whip softened butter until light and fluffy. Add remaining ingredients and mix with a wooden spoon until smooth.

For cylinders, spoon flavored butter onto plastic wrap or waxed paper in a 6-inch-long strip. Using wrap, roll butter into a 6-inch-long cylinder. Freeze for about 10 minutes, or until butter is firm enough to hold a shape. Roll mixture back and forth between 2 layers of plastic wrap to smooth. Wrap well with plastic wrap and refrigerate or freeze. When ready to use, remove wrap and slice into rounds.

For ramekins, spoon flavored butter into ramekins and smooth the top with a knife. Decorate tops with a butter stamp or create freeform designs with the tip of a knife. Or, pipe flavored butters from a pastry bag fitted with a decorative tip into ramekins.

CHOCOLATE-ALMOND DAIRY BUTTER

1/2 cup unsalted butter, softened
2 tsp. chopped toasted almonds
1/2 cup chocolate chips, melted
1/8 tsp. sugar
1 oz. almond paste, softened

CRANBERRY-ORANGE DAIRY BUTTER

1/2 cup unsalted butter, softened
1/4 cup whole-berry cranberry sauce
1/4 cup fresh orange juice
1/2 tsp. grated fresh orange peel (zest)

ORANGE-MINT DAIRY BUTTER

1/2 cup unsalted butter, softened
1 tsp. orange juice
2 tsp. grated fresh orange peel (zest)
2 tbs. chopped fresh mint, or 2 tsp. dried

LEMON-CHIVE DAIRY BUTTER

1/2 cup unsalted butter, softened
2 tsp. grated fresh lemon peel (zest)
1 tbs. fresh lemon juice
2 tbs. finely chopped fresh chives
1/2 tsp. coarsely ground black pepper

LEMON-HONEY DAIRY BUTTER

1/2 cup unsalted butter, softened
1 tsp. fresh lemon juice
1/2 tsp. grated fresh lemon peel (zest)
1 tsp. mild-flavored honey

STRAWBERRY-HONEY DAIRY BUTTER

1/2 cup unsalted butter, softened
1/2 cup fresh strawberries, hulled, crushed
1 tsp. mild-flavored honey
1/2 tsp. fresh lime or lemon juice

LIQUID INFUSIONS:
VINEGARS, LIQUEURS AND SYRUPS

PRESENTING LIQUID INFUSIONS

- Collect interesting bottles from foods you buy. Clean and sterilize them and use to present liquid infusions.

- Buy decorative bottles at swap meets, resale shops, gift shops, discount stores and kitchenware suppliers to use for homemade concoctions.

- Be sure to use snugly fitting corks or bottle caps.

- Pour flavored syrups into pretty jars or syrup servers with self-closing tops.

- Cut a rectangle of fabric large enough to cover the bottle plus a little extra to gather at the bottle's neck. If desired, cut edges with pinking shears. Tie with a pretty matching ribbon, length of colored yarn or piece of raffia at the bottle neck.

- Design a decorative label from heavy paper or card stock. List the ingredients, necessary storage information and suggested shelf life. Don't forget to write your name. Punch a hole in the corner of the label and attach it to the bottle with a ribbon. If desired, cover labels with clear tape or clear acrylic craft spray to keep them fresh looking.

- Package infusions in a gift basket along with complementary items. For example, present flavored fruit syrups with gourmet pancake mix. Or, give flavored liqueurs with homemade or purchased biscotti.

SOUTHWESTERN VINEGAR

Makes two 16-ounce bottles

This makes a delicious dressing for a salad of beans, corn and greens. If you prefer a spicier vinegar, add more chile peppers.

1 large sprig fresh rosemary
4 jalapeño or serrano chile peppers
2 tsp. capers
4 cups white wine vinegar
2 sprigs fresh rosemary, cut to jar height
4 jalapeño or serrano chile peppers
16 capers

Place 1 sprig rosemary, 4 chile peppers and 2 tsp. capers in a jar and cover with vinegar. Let sit for 2 weeks in a cool, dark place; strain. Discard solids.

Place 1 sprig rosemary, 2 chile peppers and 8 capers in each of 2 sterilized 16-ounce gift bottles (see page 6) and add strained vinegar. Close bottles tightly with corks or screw-on caps. Store in a cool, dark place for at least 1 week and up to 3 months.

MIXED HERB VINEGAR

Makes two 16-ounce bottles

On the gift enclosure, encourage the gift recipient to refill the bottle with vinegar after it is half used. Use a combination of herbs, such as mint, tarragon, chervil and marjoram.

4 tsp. chopped fresh herb leaves
3 tbs. chopped fresh chives or green onions
1 small bay leaf

2 whole cloves
4 cups white wine vinegar

Place ingredients in a jar. Cover and let sit for 1 week in a cool dark place. Strain; discard solids. Pour strained vinegar into 2 sterilized 16-ounce gift bottles. Close bottles tightly with corks or screw-on caps. Store in a cool, dark place for at least 1 week and up to 3 months.

PROVENÇAL VINEGAR

Makes two 16-ounce bottles

The herbs remain in the bottle as a pretty garnish for this flavorful vinegar.

two 4-inch-long sprigs fresh rosemary
four 3-inch-long sprigs fresh thyme

four 3-inch-long sprigs fresh sage
3½ cups white wine vinegar

Using a skewer or other long tool, gently push herbs into 2 sterilized 16-ounce gift bottles. Add vinegar and close bottles tightly with cork or screw-on caps. Store in a cool, dark place for at least 1 week and up to 3 months.

GARDEN VINEGAR

Makes two 16-ounce bottles

For a pretty presentation, leave a few inches of green tops on the carrots. Be sure to wash them carefully.

½ lemon, thinly sliced
½ lime, thinly sliced
2 thin carrots
2 string beans
1 sprig fresh parsley
3½ cups white wine vinegar

Layer lemons in the bottom of a sterilized 1-quart gift jar or wide-mouthed bottle (see page 6). Add carrots, string beans and parsley. Pour in vinegar; vegetables should float upright. Close jar tightly with a screw-on cap or cork. Store in a cool, dark place for at least 1 week and up to 3 months.

STRAWBERRY VINEGAR

Makes three 16-ounce bottles or jars

Fruit-flavored vinegars are particularly good on salads of fruits and vegetables. Try this over sliced oranges and red onions. It's also good over sliced grapefruit and shredded red cabbage.

2 pt. fresh strawberries, hulled, halved
4 cups cider vinegar
1 cup sugar

Set ½ cup of the strawberries aside. Place remaining strawberries in a large bowl with vinegar; cover and let sit for 1 hour. Place strawberry-vinegar mixture in a heavy saucepan and bring to a boil over medium-high heat. Reduce heat to low, cover and simmer for 10 minutes. Strain through a fine mesh strainer and discard solids. Cool. Pour strained mixture into sterilized gift bottles (see page 6). Add reserved strawberries. Close bottles tightly with corks or screw-on caps. Store in a cool dark place for at least 1 week and up to 3 months.

ROSEMARY VINEGAR

Makes two 16-ounce bottles

Rosemary and peppercorns give white wine vinegar a superb flavor. This is perfect for poultry marinades or over steamed vegetables.

two 5-inch-long sprigs fresh rosemary, or 2
  tsp. dried

6 whole peppercorns
4 cups white wine vinegar

Place rosemary and peppercorns in two 16-ounce sterilized gift bottles (see page 6). Add vinegar. Close bottles tightly with corks or screw-on caps. Store in a cool, dark place for a least 1 week and up to 3 months. If using dried rosemary, let solution stand for 1 week in a cool, dark place. Strain out dried herbs and replace peppercorns.

LEMON-PEPPER VINEGAR

Makes two 16-ounce bottles

This favorite combination is especially good with fish or chicken. Try it in tuna salads, also.

juice from 2 medium lemons
6 whole peppercorns

4 cups white wine vinegar
$\frac{1}{2}$ lemon, thinly sliced

Mix all ingredients together and transfer to 2 wide-necked 16-ounce sterilized gift bottles (see page 6). Close bottles tightly with corks or screw-on caps. Store in a cool, dark place for at least 1 week and up to 3 months.

ABOUT CLEAR LIQUEURS

The ingredients and equipment for making liqueurs are easily available. You will need gift bottles, a liquid measuring cup, a funnel and a strainer. All equipment should be clean and sterilized (see page 6).

Bottles should be well sealed at every stage to prevent evaporation. Use corks or screw-on metal caps with a layer of waxed paper under the cork or lid. Corks and bottle-top covers can be found at most beer and wine-making outlets and kitchen shops. Bottle-top covers are a special material that, when soaked in warm water, shrinks tightly around the bottle and cork to form a decorative seal.

Carefully label bottles to indicate the ingredients, the amount and the date on which the liqueurs were made.

Some flavorings leave sediment, which does not harm the liqueur, but it will cause the liqueur to be a bit cloudy. To eliminate cloudiness, allow the sediment to settle for a few days. Carefully pour the clear liquid into another sterilized bottle.

BASIC SUGAR SYRUP

Makes 1 cup

This forms the basis for clear liqueurs.

1 cup sugar   ½ cup water

Combine ingredients in a small saucepan. Bring to a boil over high heat and stir until all sugar is dissolved and mixture is clear. Cool before using.

FRESH ORANGE LIQUEUR

Makes two 16-ounce bottles

Since oranges are available all year, you can keep batches of orange liqueur on the shelf as gifts for any occasion.

3 cups vodka   2 whole cloves
3 whole sweet oranges, cut into wedges   1 cup Basic Sugar Syrup
½ lemon

In a wide-mouthed jar, pour vodka over oranges, lemon and cloves so that vodka completely covers fruit. Seal tightly (see page 101) and let sit in a cool, dark place for 10 days. Strain through a paper coffee filter. Discard solids. Add sugar syrup. With a funnel, pour into gift bottles. Close tightly with corks or screw-on caps. Let sit for 3 to 4 weeks before using.

ORANGE EXTRACT LIQUEUR

Makes two 16-ounce bottles

Using an extract instead of fresh fruit for flavored liqueurs gives a quick result. There's no steeping or filtering required, just a short aging period.

1½ tsp. pure orange extract
pinch cinnamon
pinch ground caraway
pinch ground coriander
3 cups vodka or brandy
1 cup Basic Sugar Syrup, page 102

Mix all ingredients in a wide-mouthed jar. Seal tightly (see page 101) and let sit in a cool, dark place for 3 days. Strain through a paper coffee filter and discard solids. With a funnel, pour liqueur into sterilized gift bottles. Close tightly with corks or screw-on caps. Let sit in a cool, dark place for 3 days.

BANANA LIQUEUR

This liqueur is perfect for an apèritif, but it's also excellent poured over ice cream and mixed into muffin, quick bread and cake batters. For crème de banane, a sweeter version of banana liqueur, double the amount of Basic Sugar Syrup. Or, split the recipe and make one portion sweeter. Use this liqueur immediately or let it mature for 2 to 3 months for a more intense flavor.

2 medium-sized firm, ripe bananas
1 tsp. vanilla extract, or one 2-inch-long vanilla bean, split (see page 5)
pinch ground cloves, optional
small stick cinnamon, optional
1 cup Basic Sugar Syrup, page 102
3 cups vodka

Mash bananas in a wide-mouthed jar and add vanilla, cloves, if using, cinnamon, if using, sugar syrup and vodka. Shake gently. Seal tightly (see page 101). Let sit in a cool, dark place for 1 week. Strain through a paper coffee filter and discard solids. Use a funnel to pour liqueur into sterilized gift bottles. Close tightly with corks or screw-on caps.

COFFEE LIQUEUR

Makes two 16-ounce bottles

Mexican Kahlua and Jamaican Tia Maria are probably the best known coffee-flavored liqueurs. They are easy to simulate at home.

2 cups distilled or filtered water
2 cups sugar
½ cup instant coffee powder
1½ cups vodka
½ vanilla bean, split (see page 5), chopped
½ tsp. caramel coloring, optional

In a saucepan, boil water with sugar until sugar is dissolved. Turn off heat. Slowly add instant coffee stir until dissolved. Cool thoroughly. In a jar, add coffee mixture to vodka with vanilla bean. Seal tightly (see page 101). Let sit in a cool, dark place for 3 weeks, shaking vigorously each day. Strain through a paper coffee filter and discard solids. Add caramel coloring if desired. Use a funnel to pour liqueur into sterilized gift bottles. Close tightly with corks or screw-on caps.

CARAWAY LIQUEUR

Makes one 16-ounce bottle

Caraway seeds are the basis for this delicious liqueur, which is also called Kummel. It is similar to aquavit, a Scandinavian distilled liqueur.

1 tbs. caraway seeds
1 whole clove
1½ cups vodka
½ cup Basic Sugar Syrup, page 102

Crush caraway seeds lightly with a mortar and pestle or on a cutting board with the bottom of a heavy pan. Place in a jar with clove and vodka. Seal tightly (see page 101). Let sit in a cool, dark place for 2 weeks. Strain through a paper coffee filter. Mix filtered mixture with sugar syrup, place in a sterilized jar and close tightly. Let sit for 1 to 6 months in a cool, dark place. Use a funnel to pour liqueur into a gift bottle. Close tightly with a cork or screw-on cap.

VARIATION: SPICED CARAWAY LIQUEUR

Add 1½ tsp. fennel or anise seeds, ¾ tsp. ground cumin and a pinch black pepper to vodka mixture with clove.

ABOUT CREAM LIQUEURS

Cream liqueurs are surprisingly simple to make. You will need a blender, measuring spoons and dark bottles to protect the milk from light, which accelerates spoiling. Cream liqueurs will keep for about 1 month when kept cold. Always refrigerate cream liqueurs, and remind the gift recipient to do so, as heat can spoil the liquid and the solutions can separate. If you don't have dark bottles, wrap light bottles with dark paper and secure with a rubber band. This will prevent the light in the refrigerator from affecting the liqueurs.

Canned milk products are safe for making cream-based liqueurs, as they have been sterilized and pasteurized to keep for indefinite periods of time. Eggs are also used to produce creamy liqueurs. However, due to the risk of contamination, many health authorities caution against using raw eggs in any food product. Pasteurized eggs or egg substitutes, which can be found in cartons in the refrigerator case of the supermarket, are safe to use in cream liqueurs.

Pay special attention when blending cream liqueurs and follow the recipes exactly. These specific instructions can make the difference between the success and failure of cream liqueurs. The main object is to minimize the amount of air you mix into the milk, cream and/or eggs. To avoid adding air to the mixture, use a "pulse-stir" method: Turn the blender on and off about 8 times during 1 minute. Make sure to use the lowest blender speed.

AMARETTO CREAM LIQUEUR

Makes three 12-ounce bottles

Using almond extract makes it easy to make a homemade version of the popular almond-flavored liqueur.

3 tsp. almond extract
1$\frac{1}{2}$ cups cognac
$\frac{1}{2}$ cup sweetened condensed milk
$\frac{1}{2}$ cup evaporated milk
$\frac{1}{2}$ cup egg substitute

In a blender on low speed, briefly blend almond extract with cognac. Add milks and pulse-stir for 1 minute (see page 107). Add egg substitute and pulse-stir for 1 minute. Using a funnel, pour mixture into dark bottles. Or, pour into light bottles and wrap with dark paper. Close tightly with corks or screw-on caps and refrigerate for up to 1 month.

DOUBLE CHOCOLATE CREAM LIQUEUR Makes two 16-ounce bottles

The chocolate lovers on your gift list will delight in the full-bodied taste of this recipe. You can also use white chocolate chips or a combination of white and dark chocolate chips.

1½ cups semisweet chocolate chips, finely chopped
2 cups Irish whiskey
3 tbs. unsweetened cocoa powder
1 cup sweetened condensed milk
½ cup egg substitute

Place ¾ cup of the chopped chocolate in a blender container. Add whiskey and cocoa powder and blend until well mixed. Add milks and pulse-stir for 1 minute (see page 107). Add egg substitute and pulse-stir for 1 minute. Add remaining chocolate chips. Using a funnel, pour mixture into dark bottles. Or, pour into light bottles and wrap with dark paper. Close tightly with corks or screw-on caps and refrigerate for up to 1 month.

MOCHA CHOCOLATE CREAM LIQUEUR Makes two 16-ounce bottles

You can toss your diet to the wind when this bottle is opened, but it's well worth it. Drink it as is or over ice, or use it on ice cream or over cream puffs. Use it in recipes, too.

1 cup very strong brewed coffee
3 tsp. chocolate syrup
1½ cups bourbon
1 cup sweetened condensed milk
1 cup light cream
½ cup egg substitute

Blend coffee, chocolate syrup and bourbon with a blender. Add milk and cream and pulse-stir for 1 minute (see page 107). Add egg substitute and pulse-stir for 1 minute. Using a funnel, pour mixture into dark bottles. Or, pour into light bottles and wrap with dark paper. Close tightly with corks or screw-on caps and refrigerate for up to 1 month.

FRESH FRUIT SYRUP

Makes two 12-ounce bottles

Fresh strawberries, cherries, blueberries and boysenberries in season work the best for this recipe, but canned and frozen berries can be used, too. Also try diced pears, peaches and plums. For a smooth syrup, press the fruit through a sieve or strainer. To serve syrup warm, heat in the microwave or immerse the bottle in a pan of hot water until warmed through.

2 cups berries or peeled diced fruit   1 cup pure maple syrup
1/4 cup sugar

Combine fruit, sugar and syrup in a small bowl. If using berries, mash them lightly with the back of a spoon until they just begin to break apart. Syrup will be chunky. Transfer mixture to sterilized gift bottles (see page 6), cover tightly with corks or screw-on caps and refrigerate for up to 1 month.

VARIATION: FAST FRUIT SYRUP

Combine 1/2 cup of your favorite fruit preserves with 1 cup pure maple syrup in a small saucepan. Cook, stirring, over medium heat until smooth and hot. Pour into a sterilized bottle and cover tightly with a cork or screw-on cap. Cool completely and store in the refrigerator for up to 1 month. Makes one 14-ounce bottle.

DRY SPICE BLENDS AND DRINK MIXES

PRESENTING DRY SPICE BLENDS AND DRINK MIXES

- Save small jars from condiments, baby foods or other items to fill with spice blends or drink mixes. Be sure to sterilize jars first (see page 6). To fill small jars easily, place mixes in a cone-shaped paper coffee filter. Snip off the bottom of the filter and use as a funnel.

- To improvise a tea bag or make a sachet, use a paper coffee filter or a double layer of cheesecloth, cut into a 5-inch square. Place 1 tbs. of the mixture in the center of the filter or cheesecloth. Pull up the edges to form a pouch and tie with colorfast twine, heavy sewing thread or dental floss. Attach a tag with the name of the gift and preparation instructions.

- Make a "set" of spice blends by packing a few different jars in a small basket or box.

- Use a vacuum sealer, plastic wrap or shrink wrap (available in craft shops) to create individual transparent bags of spices. They can be a thoughtful gift when tucked into a greeting card.

- Use a unique logo made from your name or initials that will be a reminder of your gourmet gift each time it is used.

- Be sure to attach a label to your gift that states the contents, storage and usage suggestions.

SEASONED SALT

Makes about 1⅓ cups

This makes a versatile condiment for meat or poultry.

1 cup salt
2 tsp. sugar
2 tsp. dry mustard
1½ tsp. dried oregano
1½ tsp. garlic powder

1 tsp. curry powder
1 tsp. onion powder
¼ tsp. paprika
¼ tsp. ground thyme

Mix all ingredients well. Place in sterilized gift jars (see page 6) or small bags and seal well.

HOT PEPPER SEASONING

Makes about ⅔ cup

This is a perfect gift for friends who like hot, spicy ethnic foods.

⅓ cup whole black peppercorns
2 tbs. whole white peppercorns
1 tsp. dried minced onion

3 tbs. sweet pepper flakes
1 tsp. hot red pepper flakes
½ tsp. dried minced garlic

Process all ingredients with a blender or food processor to a coarse powder. Place in sterilized gift jars (see page 6) or small bags and seal well.

HERBES DE PROVENCE

Makes cup about ½ cup

This is a traditional herb blend from the south of France. Use it to season poultry, fish, eggs and cheese. For a great gift, package it in a fancy shaker. Look for lavender in health food stores or stores that stock dried herbs in bulk.

1 tbs. dried thyme
1 tbs. dried marjoram
1 tbs. dried rosemary
1 tbs. dried basil
1 tbs. dried fennel
1 tbs. dried sage
1 tbs. dried lavender

Mix all ingredients well. Place in sterilized gift jars (see page 6) or small bags and seal well.

ITALIAN BEAN SOUP MIX
LAYERED IN A JAR

Makes about 16 servings

Pick up a few attractive jars at a resale shop; add a ribbon, flower or other customized item. Print out the recipe and attach it to the jar. Use a funnel to layer in each ingredient smoothly.

$1/2$ cup dry split peas
$1/3$ cup beef bouillon granules
$1/4$ cup pearl barley
$1/2$ cup dry lentils
$1/4$ cup dried minced onion
2 tsp. Italian seasoning
$1/2$ cup uncooked long grain rice
$1/2$ cup uncooked brown rice
$1/2$ cup alphabet macaroni or other small macaroni or tri-color spiral pasta (package this in
   a small plastic bag or wrap in colored plastic wrap).

In a 1½- to 2-pint jar, layer ingredients in the order listed. If there is space remaining at the top, fill with crushed colorful wrapping paper, a dried flower, or the printed recipe. Seal tightly. Attach the following preparation instructions to jar:

ITALIAN DRIED BEAN SOUP

- Carefully remove macaroni from top of jar and set aside.
- In a large saucepan or Dutch oven, brown 1 pound ground beef or stew meat cut into bite size pieces; drain fats.
- Add 12 cups water, one (28-ounce) can diced tomatoes and soup mix; bring to a boil.
- Reduce heat; cover and simmer for 45 minutes.
- Add pasta and simmer for 15 to 20 minutes or until macaroni, peas, lentils and barley are tender.

BASIC HERB BLEND

Makes about ¾ cup

Use this winning combination on meats, pastas and rice dishes.

3 tbs. dried basil
3 tbs. dried marjoram
3 tbs. dried thyme

3 tbs. dried tarragon
1 tbs. dried oregano
1 tbs. dried lemon peel

Mix all ingredients well. Place in sterilized gift jars (see page 6) or small bags and seal well.

CAJUN SPICE

Makes about 2 cups

Offer your friends a classic Southern spice blend to use on fish, meats and even vegetables.

¼ cup onion powder
¼ cup garlic powder
⅔ cup paprika
2 tbs. cayenne pepper

2 tbs. ground white pepper
2 tbs. ground black pepper
2 tbs. dried thyme
2 tbs. dried oregano or tarragon

Mix all ingredients well. Place in sterilized gift jars (see page 6) or small bags and seal well.

HERB SEASONING BLENDS

Makes $1/2$ to $3/4$ cup

Here are several easy-to-make customized seasoning mixtures. Mix all ingredients well. Place in sterilized gift jars (see page 6) or small bags and seal well.

HERB BLEND FOR BEEF

$1/4$ cup dried rosemary
$1/4$ cup dried parsley
2 tbs. dried minced garlic

HERB BLEND FOR LAMB

$1/4$ cup dried parsley
$1/4$ cup dried rosemary
$1/4$ cup dried marjoram

HERB BLEND FOR POULTRY

2 tbs. dried sage
2 tbs. dried thyme
2 tbs. dried marjoram
2 tbs. dried savory
2 tbs. dried rosemary

HERB BLEND FOR PORK

$1/4$ cup dried sage
$1/4$ cup dried basil
$1/4$ cup dried savory

HERB BLEND FOR FISH

$1/4$ cup dried chervil
$1/4$ cup dried parsley
$1/4$ cup dried savory

HERB BLEND FOR BEANS

$1/4$ cup dried savory
$1/4$ cup dried parsley
$1/4$ cup dried onion flakes

DRY RUBS

Makes ¼ to ¾ cup

For the following dry "marinades," mix ingredients together before placing in sterilized gift jars or small plastic bags. On the gift enclosure, tell the recipient to pierce the food with a fork in several places and rub 1 to 2 spoonfuls of the mixture over the surface of the food before grilling, roasting or broiling. For fish, use on firm varieties.

DRY RUB FOR FISH
¼ cup dried dill weed
3 tbs. paprika
¼ cup dried lemon peel
1 tsp. salt
4 tsp. freshly ground black pepper
1 tbs. cayenne pepper

DRY RUB FOR PORK
¼ cup dried thyme
2 tbs. dried sage
1 tsp. salt

2 tsp. freshly ground black pepper
1 tsp. ground allspice
½ tsp. garlic powder

DRY RUB FOR BEEF, LAMB OR CHICKEN
¼ cup dried rosemary
1 tbs. dried tarragon or basil
1½-2 tsp. dried lemon peel
2 tsp. salt
3 tsp. freshly ground black pepper
1 tbs. cumin seeds, crushed
½ tsp. garlic powder

SPICED CITRUS TEA

Makes about 1 cup dry mix; 16 servings

This recipe is delicious for instant hot tea or iced tea.

½ cup unsweetened lemon-flavored instant iced tea mix
¼ cup sugar
¼ cup orange-flavored instant breakfast drink mix
½ tsp. cinnamon
¼ tsp. ground cloves
¼ tsp. nutmeg
⅛ tsp. ground ginger

Mix all ingredients well. Place in sterilized gift jars (see page 6) or small bags and seal well.

For a single serving, pour ¾ cup boiling water over 1 tsp. spiced tea mix in a mug. Stir until dissolved.

HIBISCUS TEA

Makes about 1 cup loose tea; 16 servings

Look for hibiscus-flavored tea and hibiscus leaves in Latin American markets, specialty food stores or catalogs.

½ cup loose black or hibiscus tea
½ cup dried hibiscus leaves

2 whole cloves
½ tsp. dried lemon peel

Mix all ingredients well. Place in sterilized gift jars (see page 6), small plastic bags or tea bags (see page 113). Seal well. For a single serving, steep about 1 tbs. tea blend or 1 tea bag in boiling water for about 5 minutes. Strain if needed.

GINGER TEA

Makes about 1¼ cups loose tea; 20 servings

Ginger has a wonderful tangy taste and pleasingly pungent aroma.

1 cup loose black tea

¼ cup chopped candied ginger

Mix all ingredients well. Place in sterilized gift jars (see page 6), small plastic bags or tea bags (see page 113). Seal well. For a single serving, steep about 1 tbs. tea blend or 1 tea bag in boiling water for about 5 minutes. Strain if needed.

MULLED WINE SPICES

Makes about 1 cup dry mix; 10 to 20 servings

This recipe will flavor about 3 bottles (750 ml. each) of red or rosé wine. Try it in 2 quarts of hot cider, too. Tell the gift recipient to place spices with wine or cider in a saucepan and heat over medium-high heat to just below boiling. Reduce heat to low and continue heating for about 10 to 15 minutes. Add more sugar to taste if necessary. A thinly sliced apple and orange look and taste wonderful in the mixture. For small portions, package into a sachet (see page 113) and infuse each sachet into 2 cups hot wine or cider.

$2/3$ cup sugar
4 sticks cinnamon (4-inch pieces)
2 whole nutmegs, cracked into large pieces with a hammer
1 tbs. whole star anise
1 tsp. whole allspice
1 tsp. whole cloves
1 tbs. ground ginger

Mix all ingredients well. Place in sterilized gift jars (see page 6), plastic bags or sachets (see page 113). Seal well.

EASTERN-SPICED COFFEE

Makes 1 cup ground coffee; 8 to 10 servings

The first coffees brewed by the Turkish people contained fragrant spices and perfumes: here is a modern variation. To retain flavors, store in the refrigerator for up to 1 week or freeze.

1 cup dark-roasted coffee beans
seeds from 8 green cardamom pods
1 tsp. ground ginger

1 tsp. anise seeds or star anise pieces
8 whole black peppercorns
8 whole cloves

Mix all ingredients well. If desired, grind in a coffee grinder until fine. Place in gift jars or plastic bags. Seal well.

ALMOND-VANILLA COFFEE

Makes 1 cup ground coffee; 8 to 10 servings

This delicious combination is easy to make. It smells and tastes terrific. For best flavor, refrigerate for up to 1 week or freeze until needed.

1 cup dark-roasted coffee beans
¼ cup sliced almonds

one 8-inch-long vanilla bean, split (see page 5), cut into small pieces

Mix all ingredients well. If desired, grind in a coffee grinder until fine. Place in gift jars or plastic bags. Seal well.

SIMMERING SPICE POTPOURRI

For an inexpensive gift, purchase these ingredients in bulk from a health food or specialty food store. Package them in mason jars or a decorative jar with a tight-fitting lid. On the gift enclosure, tell the gift recipient to add about 2 tablespoons of the potpourri to 2 cups water in a small saucepan. Bring to a boil over high heat; reduce heat to low and simmer. Add more water as needed.

1½ cups cinnamon stick pieces (½-inch pieces)
1 vanilla bean, split (see page 57), cut into ½-inch pieces
½ cup whole allspice
½ cup whole cloves
½ cup bay leaves
¼ cup dried rosemary
½ cup dried orange, lemon or lime peel

Mix all ingredients well. Place in gift jars or plastic bags. Seal well.

FLAVORED HOT COCOA MIXES   Makes about 2 cups dry mix; 8 servings

Even chocolate purists will enjoy the addition of new flavors in traditional hot cocoa mix. Package in decorative jars or tins for bulk gifts. For individual packets, cut 10-inch squares of aluminum foil and place 3 tablespoons of the mix in the center. Wrap tightly to seal well. Flatten the packets and pack several in a box or basket. Be sure to label packets clearly. For individual servings, boil 3/4 cup water and stir in 3 tablespoons or 1 packet of the mix until dissolved. Look for pure vanilla powder in specialty food shops and gourmet food catalogs. Some grocery stores stock it in the baking supplies aisle.

WINTER SPICED HOT COCOA MIX
1½ cups instant hot cocoa mix
1 tbs. brown sugar
2 tbs. cinnamon
1 tbs. ground cloves
2 tsp. ground allspice
1 tsp. nutmeg

MOCHA HOT COCOA MIX
1½ cups instant hot cocoa mix
½ cup instant coffee powder or granules

VANILLA-CINNAMON HOT COCOA MIX
1½ cups instant hot cocoa mix
½ cup pure vanilla powder
2 tbs. cinnamon

MOCHA-HAZELNUT HOT COCOA MIX
1½ cups instant hot cocoa mix
½ cup hazelnut-flavored instant coffee mix

NOTE: There are many different brands of hot cocoa mix on the market. You may have to adjust the amount of cocoa per cup depending on the mix. Taste a small amount of prepared hot cocoa before packaging.

LAST-MINUTE GIFTS

PRESENTING LAST-MINUTE GIFTS

- Place chocolate-dipped cookies in a single layer in a pretty flat box. Separate cookies with double layers of waxed paper to prevent chocolate from chipping.
- Present last-minute gifts on a paper or plastic plate lined with a doily and wrapped with colored plastic wrap.
- Save plastic cottage cheese containers and use for packing small items. Wrap with foil and gather at the top. Secure with ribbon.
- Decorate plain boxes or packing paper with markers, food coloring or liquid shoe polish.
- Make a homemade "envelope" with waxed paper and place your gift inside. Use a festive ribbon to tie the gift securely and attach a fresh or dried flower or herb sprig for decoration.
- Use the box in which the cookies or graham crackers were packaged. Tape up the sides and cut a new opening on the front panel, using the back panel as the bottom. Line the entire box, inside and out, with wrapping paper or foil and place the gift inside.

BROWNIES WITH A FLAIR

Makes 16 to 20

This recipe makes dense, rich brownies. Save money by buying brownie mix in bulk from a specialty food store.

1 pkg. (8 oz.) frozen whipped dessert topping, thawed
2 eggs
1 tsp. vanilla extract
1 pkg. (1 lb., 3 oz.) brownie mix
3/4 cup chopped walnuts or pecans
1 cup semisweet or white chocolate chips
1/2 cup raisins, optional

Heat oven to 325°. Grease the bottom of an 8-inch square pan. In a large bowl, mix whipped topping, eggs and vanilla until smooth with a spoon or wire whisk. Stir in brownie mix until just moistened. Stir in nuts, 1/2 cup of the chocolate chips, and raisins, if using. Spread mixture in pan. Sprinkle remaining chocolate chips over batter. Bake for 30 to 35 minutes, until a toothpick inserted in the center comes out clean. Take care not to overbake; brownies will firm as they cool. Cool in pan and slice into bars.

CHOCOLATE-DIPPED SANDWICH WAFERS   Makes about 24

Purchased sandwich wafers with creamy centers take on a new aura when dipped in chocolates. They look fancy, but they're so easy to make. Begin with a box of chocolate and/or vanilla sandwich wafers and dip the ends in dark and white chocolate. Combine as a gift with Chocolate-Coated Graham Crackers, page 132, for variety.

24 sugar sandwich wafers
1 cup semisweet chocolate chips, melted with 2-3 tsp. vegetable oil (see page 4)
1 cup white chocolate chips, melted with 2-3 tsp. vegetable oil (see page 4)

Hold sandwich wafers with tongs and dip $1/2$ of each wafer in melted dark chocolate. Place on waxed paper to set for about 30 minutes. Carefully hold sandwich wafers on chocolate-dipped side and dip opposite side in melted white chocolate. Place on waxed paper to set for about 30 minutes.

Or, dip entire surface of wafers in dark chocolate and place on waxed paper to set for about 30 minutes. With a spoon, carefully drizzle melted white chocolate over the surface of dipped cookies in a decorative pattern.

Let chocolate set completely before packaging.

CHOCOLATE-COATED GRAHAM CRACKERS   Makes 24

If desired, you can add colored sprinkles, chocolate baci (candy worms), chopped nuts and other cake decorations to the soft chocolate before it sets. Or, create "modern art" dribbles on the crackers. If you have a steady hand, write names or draw abstract shapes on the crackers, too.

12 graham crackers, broken along perforations
1 pkg. (12 oz.) semisweet or white chocolate chips melted with 1 tsp. vegetable oil (see
   page 4), or a combination

For dipped crackers, hold each cracker by an edge with tongs and dip ½ to ¾ of it into melted chocolate. For drizzled crackers, lay plain crackers on waxed paper almost touching each other. Dip the tip of a spoon in dark chocolate and drizzle over crackers in a random pattern using a back and forth motion. Repeat with white chocolate, if using. Or, snip off a small triangle from the bottom corner of a plastic bag filled with melted chocolate and squeeze bag to drizzle chocolate over crackers.

Place chocolate-coated crackers on waxed paper for about 5 minutes, until slightly set. Refrigerate for about 30 minutes before packaging.

CRITTER COOKIES

Makes 16 to 24

The children on your gift list will love these cookie "sandwiches." Make them from tradi-tional animal crackers or other small shaped cookies, such as teddy bears or cookies shaped like Mickey Mouse. The treats will stand up by themselves and resemble a critter "family." Use any combination of ingredients and pack a variety in the gift package.

2 boxes (2⅛ oz.) animal crackers, or 1 box
  (10 oz.) Teddy Grahams
assorted jams

peanut butter
cream cheese

Sort cookies into sets of 3 identical shapes. Spread a layer of jam on one cracker and a layer of peanut butter or cream cheese on a second cracker. Assemble layers to make a three-layer cookie sandwich. Repeat with remaining crackers.

QUICK WHIMSICAL COOKIES

Use a few rolls of prepared cookie dough as a starting point for assorted whimsical cookies. Use cookie cutters or freeform shapes as the basis and decorate with items on hand in the kitchen, such as raisins, nuts, sprinkles or candies. M&Ms are a good choice. Combine different flavors of dough in the same cookie for a real treat.

1–2 pkg. (18 oz. each) refrigerated cookie dough
decorations: raisins, nuts, candies, sprinkles

Heat oven to 350°. Work with half of the dough at a time. Press or roll dough until it is 1/4-inch thick. Cut into desired shapes. To make shapes adhere to each other, press firmly on joint lines. Add lines or other details with a knife or sharp kitchen tool. Add decorations for features, buttons, etc. Placed finished shapes 2 inches apart on an ungreased baking sheet. Bake for 7 to 10 minutes, until golden brown. Cool for 1 minute; remove from baking sheet with a spatula and cool on a rack.

COOKIES ROLLING IN DOUGH

Makes 12

Bring these to your host when you're invited for brunch or lunch. They're quick to form and bake and will receive many compliments. Use any type of cookie dough.

1 can (8 oz.) refrigerated crescent rolls
$\frac{1}{2}$ pkg. (18 oz. pkg.) refrigerated cookie
   dough
$\frac{1}{2}$ cup raisins or sliced almonds

GLAZE
$\frac{2}{3}$ cup confectioners' sugar
1/8 tsp. vanilla extract
3-4 tsp. milk

Heat oven to 350°. Lightly oil a 10-inch round or square pan with nonstick cooking spray. Separate crescent roll dough into 2 long rectangles on a work surface. Overlap 2 of the long edges by $\frac{1}{2}$ inch, moistening dough edges with water and pressing together to seal well. Spoon small amounts of cookie dough evenly over surface of large rectangle. Sprinkle with raisins or almonds. Starting at one long side, roll up dough jelly roll-style. Cut roll into 12 rounds and arrange in prepared pan cut-sides up. Bake for 25 to 28 minutes, until golden brown. Cool for 15 minutes. In a small bowl, combine glaze ingredients and drizzle over warm rolls. To reheat, wrap with foil and warm in a 325° oven for about 5 minutes.

PRICKLY BEAR BISCUITS

Makes 6

Send these to school for a child's birthday party. Shape packaged biscuit dough into the head of a teddy bear—add raisins for facial features. Let the children help make them.

1 can (11.3 oz.) refrigerated dinner rolls
$1/2$ cup sesame seeds or sunflower kernels
36 raisins
1 egg white mixed with 1 tbs. water

Heat oven to 400°. Spray a baking sheet with nonstick spray or line with foil. Separate dough into 8 portions. Roll 6 of the dough portions into balls and roll balls in seeds until completely covered. Flatten balls slightly on prepared baking sheet to form bears' "heads." Separate remaining 2 dough portions into halves. Cut 3 of the halves in half to form 6 portions. Shape each sixth into 2 semicircular "ears" and attach to top sides of large circles using egg white mixture to adhere. Separate remaining dough into 6 small balls and press into the center of each head to form a "nose." Press raisins in dough to form "eyes," "nostrils" and "ear centers." Place 2 inches apart on baking sheet and bake for 8 to 10 minutes, until light golden brown.

FRUIT- AND CHEESE-FILLED BISCUITS

Makes 10

Begin with refrigerated buttermilk biscuit dough, add an easy fruit and cheese filling and the result is a sweet roll that resembles a wheel.

4 oz. cream cheese, softened
1/4 cup strawberry jelly
1/2 cup raisins
2 cans (10 biscuits each) refrigerated
  buttermilk biscuits

GLAZE
2/3 cup confectioners' sugar
1/8 tsp. vanilla extract
3-4 tsp. milk

Heat oven to 375°. Grease a large baking sheet. In small bowl, combine cream cheese, jelly and raisins and blend well. Separate dough into 20 portions and flatten each portion into a 4-inch circle. Place 10 of the circles on prepared baking sheet. Divide cheese mixture among dough portions. Top filled dough portions with remaining unfilled dough portions, lining up the edges. Press edges together with a fork to seal. Cut five 1/2-inch-long slits in the top of each filled biscuit in a decorative manner to allow steam to escape. Bake for 15 to 20 minutes, until golden brown. Cool for 15 minutes.

In a small bowl, combine Glaze ingredients and drizzle over warm biscuits. To reheat, wrap with foil and warm in a 325° oven for about 5 minutes.

APPLE-RAISIN ROLLUPS

Makes 8

Your friends will enjoy the taste and texture of soft, steamy apples baked within crescent rolls.

1 can (8 oz.) refrigerated crescent rolls
1 medium-sized red apple, thinly sliced
$\frac{1}{4}$ cup raisins
cinnamon

Heat oven to 350°. Separate crescent roll dough into 8 triangles and lay on a foil-lined baking sheet. Place 1 apple slice on each dough triangle. Sprinkle each portion evenly with raisins and a touch of cinnamon. Roll up dough securely starting at the wide end and place point-side down on pan. Bake for 12 to 15 minutes, until golden brown. Watch carefully so rollups do not burn.

BLUEBERRY CRESCENTS

Makes 8

These blueberry-filled rolls are reminiscent of French croissants. However, they are much easier to make.

1 can (8 oz.) refrigerated crescent rolls
1 cup fresh blueberries

Heat oven to 350°. Separate crescent roll dough into 8 triangles and lay on a foil-lined baking sheet. Place a few blueberries near the wide end of each triangle. Roll up dough securely starting at the wide end and place point-side down on pan. Curve the ends in a crescent shape. Bake for 12 to 15 minutes, until golden brown. Watch carefully so crescents do not burn.

BREADSTICK STARTERS

Makes 8

Most packaged breadsticks are covered with salt. When you make them from packaged refrigerated dough, you can be more inventive with your toppings. Before baking, roll the breadstick dough in your favorite coating. Vary the coatings for a scrumptious gift basket.

1 pkg. (8 oz.) refrigerated breadstick dough
coatings: sesame seeds, caraway seeds, garlic salt, Basic Herb Blend, page 118, or other
   flavorings

Remove dough from package and separate into portions. Place desired coating on a piece of waxed paper. Roll each dough portion in coating so that it is completely covered. Place coated dough a few inches apart on an ungreased baking sheet. Bake according to package directions.

INSTANT GIFT IDEAS

When time constraints prevent you from creating incredible edibles from scratch, you can still arrive at your destination with a package of goodies. Combine items from your kitchen or purchase packaged items from the market and assemble them imaginatively. Grab a lovely bottle, jar, bowl, cocktail glass, candy tin or basket. Take along some wrappings and stuffings, too. Stop on the way to your party to pick up a package of cheese, a small salami, jars of fruit spreads, boxes of candy or countless other items and wrap them up to make a special package.

If you're in this gift-making bind often, save food catalogs from the holidays along with your wrapping supplies. They'll spark ideas. Of course, you can buy gift packages ready-made, but that's neither as much fun nor as personal as selecting each item yourself!

- Layer different types of rice in a bottle. If the kernels tend to mix, be sure the varieties have the same cooking time. Or, cut a layer of waxed paper the shape of the bottle to divide the rice varieties. Look for arborio, jasmine, basmati, wild or other types of rice for a beautiful gift.

- Layer various shapes and colors of pastas in a bottle, separated into sections.

- Layer different types of dried beans in a bottle, jar or glass. Attach a few of your favorite bean recipes on cards or include a small recipe book. Select beans with different colors, such as adzuki, anasasi, cannellini, red and black beans.

- Pack an assortment of wrapped cheese with a box of crackers and a bottle of wine in a basket. Wrap the basket with clear plastic wrap.
- Arrange packages of assorted teas and coffees on a pretty tray and wrap decoratively.
- Give a basket of fresh fruits with packages of whole nuts. Add a set of fruit knives and a novelty nutcracker if desired.
- Give jars of jelly or chutney with packages of crackers and cheese.
- Present mixed dried fruits, such as peaches, apricots, raisins, pears, cherries, mangoes or pineapple rings in a covered glass jar. Tie with a ribbon.
- Give purchased candy with liqueurs in baskets or small wooden boxes.
- Present assorted bags of hard candies in a "trick or treat" bag or basket.
- Purchase an assortment of French pastries from a local bakery. Present them in the classic pink pastry box that many bakeries use. As soon as your recipient sees that pink box, he or she will know a special treat awaits.

PACKAGING GOURMET GIFTS

CREATIVE PACKAGING

An interesting-looking package heightens the anticipation of opening it. Use creative containers, stuffings, wrappings, ties and ribbons, decorations, tags and labels to enhance your gourmet gifts. With a little imagination, the container can become as great a treasure as its contents. Scores of ideas follow, but don't be afraid to make up your own.

CONTAINERS: Make the container a gift item, too. The gift recipient will remember your thoughtfulness long after the food has been enjoyed.

- baking pans
- baskets
- decorative bottles
- canisters
- champagne buckets
- unused Chinese food take-out containers
- foil or paper candy cups
- cigar or pencil boxes
- coffee mugs
- pretty drinking glasses and vases
- hat boxes
- jewelry boxes
- mason jars
- sand pails
- plastic pint berry baskets
- garden-tool carriers
- wine-bottle carriers
- cookie or candy tins

WRAPPINGS AND STUFFINGS: There are many things you can use to wrap and stuff gifts in addition to purchased wrapping paper and tissue paper.

- homemade wrapping paper(see pages 147-149)
- aluminum foil
- decorated brown paper bags
- calendar pages
- clear or colored plastic wrap
- fabrics, such as gingham, denim, chintz or lace
- printed dishtowels
- netting
- plain paper decorated with colored markers or finger paints
- road maps
- sheet music
- travel posters
- leftover wallpaper
- shredded tissue paper
- printed cocktail napkins

TIES AND RIBBONS: Use these ideas to adorn boxes, baskets and bottles. Some can even become part of the gift.

- braids, cording and fringe from a fabric store
- strings of beads, shells or seeds
- men's neckties
- women's scarves
- raffia
- wire-edged ribbons
- lace trim

OTHER PACKAGE TOPPERS: Use a glue gun, floral wire or clear tape to attach other kinds of decorative items to your gifts.

- small kitchen items, such as measuring spoons, peelers, bottle stoppers and corn holders
- fresh or dried flowers
- dried berries, nuts or pine cones
- silky tassels
- paper fans
- whimsical toys, such as little cars, whistles or alphabet blocks
- small ornaments
- tiny baskets
- miniature dolls
- seashells
- sequins
- decorative buttons
- felt shapes
- beads

TAGS AND LABELS: For many gifts it is necessary to attach tags citing the contents, storage and reheating suggestions. You'll also want a tag stating both the name of the giver and receiver. Punch a hole in the tag and tie it on the package if necessary.

- ready-made tags from stationery and kitchen shops
- shapes cut from old greeting cards
- customized computer labels
- place cards
- heavy paper cut into shapes
- recipe cards that say "From the Kitchen of..."

HOMEMADE WRAPPING PAPER

Turn ordinary paper into unique gift wrap with imprints or stencils. Embellish plain paper, printed paper, brown paper bags or even ribbons. Print on card stock, too, to use for tags and labels. You can even make an image directly on a plain box and skip the wrapping paper. Acrylic paints, finger paints and colored ink pads can be used for imprinting. You can use the same printing techniques for imprinting fabric, but use fabric paints instead. Spray paint is used for stenciling.

FRUIT AND VEGETABLE IMPRINTS

Select fruits and vegetables that have a distinctive shape. Small items are easier to use for imprints than large items. Try fresh chile peppers, bell peppers, artichokes, mushrooms, broccoli, cauliflower, baby carrots, potatoes, crabapples or persimmons.

1. Make a smooth, flat cut through the vegetable or fruit to create a flat surface for imprinting.

2. Place a palette of acrylic paints on a paper plate. Place enough paint on the plate to accommodate the surface of the imprinting item. For larger items, spread the paint on the imprinting surface with a foam brush.

3. Gently press the paint-coated object on the paper, card stock or ribbon you wish to

decorate. You'll get about three imprints per "inking." Be careful not to apply too much paint on the object, to avoid getting paint on your fingers.

HERB IMPRINTS

An herb sprig can be imprinted by pressing the sprig firmly on an ink pad. You can hold the herb sprig with waxed paper to prevent touching the ink with your hands. Place the inked herb sprig on the item you wish to decorate and, using a clean sheet of waxed paper, press the inked sprig firmly on the paper, card stock or ribbon. For extra impact, attach a fresh sprig of the same herb under the ribbon of the gift.

FISH VERTEBRAE AND BONE IMPRINTS

Save the vertebrae from a small cooked whole fish and carefully pull it away from the flesh. Wash vertebrae and let dry thoroughly. Dip the vertebrae in acrylic paint or finger paints and carefully lay it on the item you wish to decorate. Place waxed paper over the vertebrae and weigh it down with a book for a minute or two. Round steak bones, marrow bones or other interestingly shaped bones make wonderful stamp designs. Their organic shapes offer a more intriguing look than perfect geometric shapes. And, should you mess up one or two, they're forgivable.

LEAF IMPRINTS

Select leaves with an interesting shape. Using a small foam rubber brush, cover the surface of the leaf with paint, working it into the veins. Carefully lay the painted side of the leaf on the object you wish to decorate. Repeat the process with 3 or 4 leaves, being cautious not to move the leaves as you proceed. Gently lay a sheet of waxed paper over the leaves. Place a heavy book on the waxed paper to weigh down the leaves for a minute or two. Carefully remove the book and waxed paper, taking care not to smear the paint. Repeat until the surface of the paper, box or other item is covered.

STENCILS

A variety of precut stencils are available in craft shops in small, inexpensive booklets or as individual designs. You can also make your own stencils by cutting stencil paper, available from art and craft material suppliers, with a craft knife into the desired shapes. Things you find in nature, such as sturdy, flat leaves and flower petals, can be used as a stencil as well.

Lay stencils in a decorative pattern over the object you wish to decorate. With spray paint, spray a fine mist over stencils, taking care not to disturb them. Allow paint to dry and gently lift off stencils. Don't worry if the design is not perfect — it adds character.

PACKING AND SHIPPING SUGGESTIONS

Packaging your gifts for shipping should be part of the planning behind giving a gift. Following these suggestions will keep everyone happy.

- Wrap cookies, bars and exposed foods with plastic wrap or small plastic bags to keep them fresh and to avoid contact with packaging materials. Keep gifts snug in their container by gently stuffing the container with waxed paper, tissue paper or popcorn, which serve as lightweight cushioning materials. Do not send highly perishable foods unless you can ensure they will be constantly refrigerated.

- Wrap bottles and other fragile containers in bubble wrap, plastic foam or similar wrapping materials. "Double box" these items, which means placing them in a sturdy box inside another sturdy box with cushioned packaging materials between the boxes.

- Do not use masking, duct or narrow transparent tape, which are not strong enough to handle rough shipping conditions. Choose strong plastic, water-activated or reinforced packing tape that is at least 2 inches wide. You can buy such products at a post office or packaging store.

- Do not use string or rope to secure packages, as they can catch on various conveyer racks used by shipping companies.

- Use a new corrugated cardboard box rather than an old flimsy one. If you do reuse a box, be sure to remove all old labels and bar codes.

- Label packages properly. Always include the receiver's ZIP code with complete street address, including apartment numbers when applicable. For rural or post office boxes, include a phone number. Always double check when copying numbers from an address book to a label.

- Place one address label on top of the box. Placing labels on more than one side of the box will only confuse the mailing service.

- Always include your full return address and ZIP code on the outside of the package. Avoid putting labels over seams or box closure areas. Always include a copy of the gift recipient's address and your return address inside the parcel.

- Allow ample time for the package to arrive. Mailing services offer different prices for various mailing options. Plan ahead to get the best deal

- If you're not sure about any aspect of packaging and shipping, call the shipping company's customer service line for information. Or, take your gift to a local pack and ship store. They are experts on packing fragile goods and offering the best shipping options for different types of packages.

INDEX

Serve Creative, Easy, Nutritious Meals with nitty gritty® Cookbooks

1 or 2, Cooking for
100 Dynamite Desserts
9 x 13 Pan Cookbook
Bagels, Best
Barbecue Cookbook
Beer and Good Food
Blender Drinks
Bread Baking
Bread Machine
Bread Machine II
Bread Machine III
Bread Machine V
Bread Machine VI
Bread Machine, Entrees
Burger Bible
Cappuccino/Espresso
Casseroles
Chicken, Unbeatable
Chile Peppers
Clay, Cooking in
Coffee and Tea
Convection Oven

Cook-Ahead Cookbook
Crockery Pot, Extra-Special
Deep Fryer
Dehydrator Cookbook
Edible Gifts
Edible Pockets
Fabulous Fiber Cookery
Fondue and Hot Dips
Fondue, New International
Fresh Vegetables
Freezer, 'Fridge, Pantry
Garlic Cookbook
Grains, Cooking with
Healthy Cooking on Run
Ice Cream Maker
Indoor Grill, Cooking on
Italian Recipes
Juicer Book II
Kids, Cooking with Your
Kids, Healthy Snacks for
Loaf Pan, Recipes for
Low-Carb Recipes

Lowfat American
No Salt No Sugar No Fat
Party Foods/Appetizers
Pasta Machine Cookbook
Pasta, Quick and Easy
Pinch of Time
Pizza, Best
Porcelain, Cooking in
Pressure Cooker, Recipes
Rice Cooker
Rotisserie Oven Cooking
Sandwich Maker
Simple Substitutions
Skillet, Sensational
Slow Cooking
Slow Cooker, Vegetarian
Soups and Stews
Soy & Tofu Recipes
Tapas Fantásticas
Toaster Oven Cookbook
Waffles & Pizzelles
Wraps and Roll-Ups

**For a free catalog, call: Bristol Publishing Enterprises
(800) 346-4889
www.bristolpublishing.com**